AF323433

BEYOND THE
BRI

Can India, Japan and the US
Provide an Alternative Model
of Connectivity?

BEYOND THE BRI

Can India, Japan and the US Provide an Alternative Model of Connectivity?

Rupakjyoti Borah

Dr Vishwanath Karad MIT-World Peace University, India

World Scientific

NEW JERSEY · LONDON · SINGAPORE · BEIJING · SHANGHAI · HONG KONG · TAIPEI · CHENNAI

Published by

World Scientific Publishing Co. Pte. Ltd.

5 Toh Tuck Link, Singapore 596224

USA office: 27 Warren Street, Suite 401-402, Hackensack, NJ 07601

UK office: 57 Shelton Street, Covent Garden, London WC2H 9HE

Library of Congress Control Number: 2024046643

British Library Cataloguing-in-Publication Data
A catalogue record for this book is available from the British Library.

BEYOND THE BRI
Can India, Japan and the US Provide an Alternative Model of Connectivity?

ISBN 978-981-98-0556-3 (hardcover)
ISBN 978-981-98-0557-0 (ebook for institutions)
ISBN 978-981-98-0558-7 (ebook for individuals)

For any available supplementary material, please visit
https://www.worldscientific.com/worldscibooks/10.1142/14108#t=suppl

Desk Editors: Aanand Jayaraman/Venkatesh Sandhya

Typeset by Stallion Press
Email: enquiries@stallionpress.com

Foreword

In an era marked by rapid globalisation and unprecedented technological advancements, the imperative for robust and interconnected infrastructure has never been more urgent. The world is witnessing a transformative shift, driven by urbanisation, industrialisation and the rising aspirations of billions. Yet, the global infrastructure landscape remains fragmented, plagued by disparities and geopolitics and often dominated by unsustainable practices.

Professor Borah's timely and insightful analysis in *Beyond the BRI: Can India, Japan and the US Provide an Alternative Model of Connectivity?* provides a much-needed roadmap for navigating these complex challenges. The book offers a comprehensive examination of the critical role that infrastructure plays in fostering economic growth, social development and environmental sustainability.

Drawing upon his extensive research and firsthand experience, Professor Borah underscores the urgent need for a unified approach among major democratic powers. China's Belt and Road Initiative (BRI), while ambitious, has often raised concerns regarding its opaque financing practices, environmental impact and potential debt traps. A values-driven, transparent and sustainable alternative is essential to counterbalance China's influence and promote a more equitable and prosperous world.

The book delves into the intricate challenges and opportunities facing India, Japan and the United States in forging such a partnership. It explores the potential synergies between these countries, their existing collaborations and the areas where they can leverage their respective strengths. Professor Borah's analysis is grounded in a deep understanding of the geopolitical, economic and social factors that shape infrastructure development.

The book also addresses the challenges that may hinder the implementation of a unified approach, such as geopolitical tensions, differing economic priorities and domestic political considerations. He suggests strategies for overcoming these obstacles and building consensus among key stakeholders.

In addition to the challenges and opportunities, Professor Borah explores the critical role of technology in shaping the future of global infrastructure. Advancements in areas such as artificial intelligence, big data and the Internet of Things (IoT) offer unprecedented opportunities for enhancing efficiency, sustainability and resilience. By leveraging these technologies, we can optimise infrastructure planning, improve asset management and develop innovative solutions to address pressing challenges.

By examining the specific needs and priorities of developing countries, the book offers a pragmatic and actionable framework for a global infrastructure initiative. It highlights the importance of sustainable financing, technological innovation and capacity building in ensuring the long-term success of such endeavours.

Moreover, Professor Borah's emphasis on environmental sustainability and social equity is a refreshing departure from the narrow focus on economic growth. The book underscores the critical role of infrastructure in addressing climate change, reducing poverty and promoting social justice.

In conclusion, *Beyond the BRI: Can India, Japan and the US Provide an Alternative Model of Connectivity?* is a timely and thought-provoking contribution to the discourse on global development. Professor Borah's insightful analysis and practical recommendations offer a valuable guide for policymakers, practitioners and academics alike. By understanding the challenges and opportunities that lie ahead, we can work together to build a more interconnected, sustainable and equitable world.

Subba Rao Duvvuri
Governor (2008–2013)
Reserve Bank of India

Preface

This book seeks to take a look at what are the alternate connectivity projects which are being offered or are on the anvil as China's signature initiative, the BRI (or the Belt and Road Initiative), has taken up pace in countries across the world. The BRI is the most ambitious project that has been launched by China in modern times. It derives from the ancient Silk Road which helped China reach out to different parts of the world. As a part of the same, China has been reaching out to countries both in the immediate neighbourhood and beyond. Some of the countries like the Central Asian countries had already been close to China and these ties have only got stronger in the last couple of years.

However, this is not without problems either. In the last couple of years, especially after the outbreak of COVID-19, growth has slowed down globally. In addition, the priorities of the Chinese government are different now from what was the case 10 years back.

This book takes into account the present geopolitical situation in the world as a lot of these projects (as a part of the BRI) depend on the geopolitical and geo-economic situation. It looks at the possibility of providing sustainable alternatives to various countries when it comes to the environment.

It also develops some futuristic scenarios and looks at what could happen in case of a sudden outbreak of some kind of a pandemic or in case the situation worsens due to the fighting in the Middle East. Besides, the Russia–Ukraine conflict shows no signs of abating and this is not good news for the infrastructure sector across the world.

Chapter 1 deals with China's rationale behind the BRI — as to why Beijing has invested so much money and resources into the BRI and what is the bigger game plan that China has in mind. It looks at what is the BRI all about. It shows why China started the BRI in the first place and what was the original rationale for the same. While the initial reasons may have been different, things have changed, especially with the onset of COVID-19.

Chapter 2 deals with why India has not joined the BRI. India is one of the major countries which has not joined the BRI, along with countries like Japan and the United States. It looks at what are the gains and losses for India as the BRI makes progress, especially in the immediate neighbourhood with countries like Bangladesh, Pakistan, Nepal and Maldives having joined the BRI bandwagon.

Chapter 3 deals with the experience of countries which have joined the China-led BRI. It looks at how various countries have dealt with and responded to the BRI, both in Asia and also in continents like Europe. It looks at the impact of BRI on other countries, which include countries in Africa, Latin America and others. One important example is that of Sri Lanka. It joined the BRI and after that took copious amounts of loans from China and soon, however, it was mired in debt. When Sri Lanka could not pay back the loan amount, it had to give away the Hambantota Port to a China-led consortium and also close to 15,000 acres of land around the port for a Special Economic Zone. Another important example is that of Laos, which has built a high-speed railway with Chinese loans, but it has put a huge pressure on the Laotian economy. Again, in some African countries where the projects have actually become operational, there are many issues at stake.

Chapter 4 deals with the connectivity initiatives which have been launched by countries (other than China) across the world. While one of them is the Build Back Better World initiative (which has been initiated by the G7 countries), there are others too in the works, like the IMEC (India–Middle East Economic Corridor).

Chapter 5 is the concluding chapter which talks about how India, Japan and the United States can offer a viable alternative to the China-led BRI. While there are many individual projects being developed across the world, there is no over-arching project that can take on the BRI. It also looks at which are the countries that can provide an alternative. The United States is of course the leader since it is the leading economy in the world.

At the same time, Japan has a Free and Open Indo-Pacific Vision (FOIP) which started from the time of the former Japanese PM Shinzo Abe.

The main idea of this book is to analyse the 10-year journey of the China-led BRI (Belt and Road Initiative) since its inception in 2013 and look at the successes and the failures of the same. At the same time, the book looks at if any alternative options can be provided collectively by India, Japan and the US when it comes to the infrastructure front. It also looks at the impact of the coronavirus pandemic on the infrastructure sector, in countries across the world. Finally, it charts out a roadmap for the growth of infrastructure in countries across the world, both as a part of the China-led BRI and otherwise.

About the Author

Prof(Dr) Rupakjyoti Borah is Professor and Dean-in-Charge at The School of Liberal Arts (SOLA), Dr Vishwanath Karad MIT-World Peace University, Pune. He has served as Visiting Professor at Gakushuin University, in Tokyo, Japan. In addition, he has successfully completed visiting assignments at the University of Cambridge (UK), the Australian National University (Australia), the Japan Institute of International Affairs (Japan) and the National University of Singapore (NUS).

He holds a PhD from the School of International Studies, Jawaharlal Nehru University (JNU), India.

He is a Young Strategists' Forum 2019 Alumni (organised by the German Marshall Fund of the US-GMFUS). He was also a speaker at the Jakarta International Defence Dialogue on "Building Maritime Collaboration for Security and Stability" along with the likes of Admiral Harry B Harris, former commander of the US Pacific Command. He has published in Scopus-indexed journals like *The Roundtable — The Commonwealth Journal of International Affairs* and the *Australian Journal of International Affairs*.

This is his fourth book. His other books are *The Strategic Relations between India, the United States and Japan in the Indo-Pacific: When Three is Not a Crowd* (2021), *Act-East via the Northeast-How India's Northeast is Strengthening the Kizuna (bond) between India, Japan and ASEAN?* (2019) and *The Elephant and the Samurai: Why Japan Can Trust India?* (2017).

Acknowledgements

A host of people have helped me in the process of writing this book.

First and foremost, I would like to thank my wife, Maushumi, and my sons, Hurjyudoy and Bishwabhiraj, who with their utmost patience have always stood by me. My wife's smile and my younger son's hugs helped me a lot as I took on this onerous task amidst a whole lot of other responsibilities. I would also like to thank my mother, Mrs. Chitra Borah.

In India, I would like to thank my office colleagues who helped me and Prof. Santosh Kumar, my former Dean, who has always encouraged me to aim higher. I would also like to thank Dr. Duvvuri Subbarao, former Governor of the Reserve Bank of India who has very kindly agreed to write the foreword of this book.

In Japan, I would like to thank Prof. Michimi Muranushi and the Gakushuin University in Tokyo, which awarded me a Visiting Fellowship during February and March 2024. My stay of 2 months in Tokyo, Japan, allowed me to complete major portions of this book. Thanks also due to Prof. Tomohiko Taniguchi-sensei for his invaluable time and advice. I would also like to thank Go Yamada-san for always being very helpful during my many visits to Japan. I would also like to thank Maki Aobe-san of IDE-JETRO for her valuable insights. Thanks are also due to Suzuki-san of the JETRO office in New Delhi. In addition, I would also like to thank Yuichi Koshikawa-san, Section Chief of EOI Section 2, International Operation Division, National Taxation Agency, Japan, and Masayuki Kameda-san, Ministry of Foreign Affairs (MoFA), Government of Japan, for their kind help and ideas when it comes to India–Japan ties and life in

Japan in general. Thanks are also due to Susan Komori-san and Yasuo Naito-san in Japan.

In Russia, I would like to thank my close friend, Svetlana, who has always been there, in times, both good and bad.

Thanks are also due to my publishers at World Scientific, Singapore, the proof checkers and a whole lot of people from the publication team, for sticking to a tight schedule.

Finally, this book is dedicated to my late father, who helped me to understand what "connectivity" is all about by taking me for rides all over the country.

Last, but not the least, I take full responsibility for any mistakes that I have committed in this book of mine and ask for your forgiveness.

Contents

Chapter 1

China's Rationale behind the BRI

The Belt and Road Initiative (BRI), also known within China as the "One Belt One Road", is an ambitious Chinese government initiative which began in 2013. As part of the same, China plans to invest/has invested in more than 150 countries and international organizations. Widely seen as the brainchild of Chinese President Xi Jinping, it forms a central part of President Xi's "Major Country Diplomacy" strategy, which aims for a bigger role for China in global affairs. As per Beijing, 155 countries have signed up to the BRI which roughly corresponds to almost 75% of the world's population and more than half of the world's GDP.

The BRI is composed of two distinct segments — the "Silk Road Economic Belt" which refers to the overland routes for road and rail transportation to Europe from China through landlocked Central Asia, whereas "Road" refers to the "21st Century Maritime Silk Road" and the Indo-Pacific sea routes through Southeast Asia to South Asia, the Middle East and Africa. A host of infrastructure projects are a part of the BRI which include ports, buildings, railroads, roads, bridges, airports, dams, coal-fired power stations and railroad tunnels. The BRI is expected to be complete by 2049, which will coincide with the centennial of China's founding.

It is worth noting here that, India, Japan and the US have not joined the Beijing-backed BRI. At the same time, Japan has the "Partnership for Quality Infrastructure" initiative, which aims at developing high-quality infrastructure across the world. The growing collaboration between Japan and India in the infrastructure realm assumes significance in the light of

Japan's "Free and Open Indo-Pacific Vision" and India's "Act-East Policy".

It has been estimated that India will need around US$4.5 trillion by 2040 for the development of its infrastructure sector.[1] Japan has been disbursing Official Development Assistance (ODA) to India for a long time, with the first tranche of Japanese ODA coming way back in 1958. It is worth noting here that Japan is the largest bilateral donor to India. Japanese ODA has been helping India in areas like power, transportation, environmental projects and projects related to basic human needs.

Some of the major projects being executed with Japanese ODA in India include the Ahmedabad–Mumbai High-Speed Rail Project, the Western Dedicated Freight Corridor (DFC), the Delhi–Mumbai Industrial Corridor with 12 new industrial townships and the Chennai–Bengaluru Industrial Corridor (CBIC) besides the flagship Delhi Metro project.

The Mumbai–Ahmedabad high-speed railway project will be key for both Japan and India since Tokyo has been trying to export its railway technology to other parts of the world while New Delhi is trying to upgrade its railways from the colonial-era system. Another important aspect of New Delhi's growing ties with Tokyo has been the burgeoning cooperation between Japan and Northeast India.

Already countries like the US and the G7 countries are working on alternate mechanisms to bolster infrastructure development. In June 2021, G7 partners agreed to launch a new global infrastructure initiative, "the Build Back Better World (B3W) initiative, a values-driven, high-standard, and transparent infrastructure partnership to help narrow the US$40+ trillion infrastructure need in the developing world".[2]

Another important factor in the case of the BRI is the demographic factor as China is grappling with decreasing population. There are many parts of China where the population is decreasing very fast and hence many ghost cities have emerged.

---

[1] *The Economic Times*, https://m.economictimes.com/news/economy/infrastructure/india-will-need-usd-4-5-trillion-till-2040-for-infra-development-amitabh-kant/article-show/66445530.cms.

[2] White House, Fact Sheet: President Biden and G7 Leaders Launch Build Back Better World (B3W) Partnership, available at https://www.whitehouse.gov/briefing-room/statements-releases/2021/06/12/fact-sheet-president-biden-and-g7-leaders-launch-build-back-better-world-b3w-partnership/.

There are a host of factors on which the BRI is dependent. These include the change of governments. For example, there has been a change in governments, in the case of countries like Nepal or say Maldives and this has changed the momentum of the progress of the BRI.

In addition, what has happened is that there is information about locals pocketing bribes or kickbacks in the contracts which have been awarded as a part of the BRI and this is a grave challenge.

Terrorism is another challenge as seen in the context of Sri Lanka which saw the Easter attacks in 2019. The going has never been the same in Sri Lanka after that. It is worth mentioning here that Sri Lanka had signed on to the BRI and has been an integral part of the same.

Why Did China Start the BRI?

China started the BRI for a host of reasons.

First, one major reason is falling demand at home and a desire to reach out to new markets both in Asia as well as Europe. Due to a rapid fall in birth rates, China has a serious lack of demand at home. In addition, the property market has collapsed and without Chinese companies, expanding into the global market, they cannot earn much profits. This is similar to what Japanese companies did in the 1970s and later.

Second, the Chinese government's rationale for the BRI is also to spread its influence and to generate employment for its citizens since in many of the projects, only Chinese labourers have got employment as has happened in some of the African countries. At the same time, this has led to a lot of problems in some of the African countries and conflicts with the local authorities.

The Chinese government realised that sooner or later, it would run into problems with the US on the economic front. Hence, one way of overcoming this is to enter into economic ties with other nations. Already we have seen that in the aftermath of Russia's war with Ukraine, the biggest beneficiary has been China since the Western countries have slapped Russia and Russian entities with a host of sanctions and there is no alternative for Russia but to do business with China.

Third, in addition, China has been trying to boost economic links to its less developed western parts of the country unlike the eastern parts of the country. The western Chinese province of Xinjiang has seen large-scale violence in the past and the Chinese authorities have cracked down in a heavy-handed manner. In addition, China has also expanded trade links to the Central Asian countries which have ethnic links to the Uighur people of Xinjiang. One of the biggest outreach that China has done when it comes to the BRI is to the Central Asian countries. The main reason for the same is that China wants to reduce any kind of support to the Uighurs from the Central Asian countries which are ethnically related to the Uighurs. In addition, the Central Asian countries have a lot of energy resources and the Chinese economy is in dire need of the same.

Fourth, with this, Chinese President Xi Jinping wants to carve out a legacy for himself, both within China and the wider world. It is also worth noting that Xi Jinping had been elected as President for a third term, thereby making him the strongest Chinese leader after Mao Zedong. The cult of personality has always been very strong in China and Xi Jinping is no exception. He would also like to leave a legacy not only in China but also in other parts of the world where the BRI has made inroads.

Another reason could be that there is an internal power struggle that is going on within China and in this Xi Jinping wants to overcome other contenders. He already is the most powerful leader in recent history. Chinese President Xi Jinping has already fired his Foreign Minister Qin Gang and two top leaders of its People's Liberation Army Rocket Force (PLARF), which handles the Chinese nuclear arsenal. This clearly shows that not all is well on the domestic front. In addition, the central government has called on the country's richest provinces — Guangdong, Jiangsu, Zhejiang, Shandong, Henan and Sichuan — which account for roughly 40% of economic output to help the other provinces.

Fifth, it could also be a ploy to ensnare countries into a kind of debt trap as has already happened in the case of countries like Sri Lanka. These countries are important for China in a host of ways. For example, Sri Lanka lies directly at the heart of sea lanes of communication in the Indian Ocean region and hence its location is very important. It seems that China has specifically been targeting those countries whose geopolitical location is crucial and this includes countries like Sri Lanka and also countries like Cambodia in Southeast Asia. Through Cambodia what China has done is that it has created divisions within the ASEAN and this certainly helps in its long-term game.

Sixth, the BRI is in many ways a geopolitical construct. China has been aiming to dominate the sea lanes of traffic in the Indian Ocean region for a long term now. Beijing has always been eyeing the warm water ports in the region since it relies on the import of energy resources and the export of finished goods. China has built or is in the process of building a series of ports in the region, which are collectively known as the "String of Pearls". These include ports like Gwadar in Pakistan, Kyaukpyu Port in Myanmar and Hambantota in Sri Lanka. Some Indian and Western scholars have opined that the Chinese would like to make the Indian Ocean a "Chinese lake." They are already a big presence in the South China Sea region and a foothold on the Indian Ocean would make them very powerful.

China would also like to reduce the American influence across the world and many of the ports are being built by Chinese state-owned companies. In times of war, these could be used by Chinese authorities and this is a threat that countries like India, US and Japan cannot ignore. These "dual-use" ports have sprung up all over the world and what is even more worrying is that China has signed agreements with some of the local agreements allowing these ports to be used by so-called Chinese research ships, etc.

In addition, China is also trying to open a land route to Europe via the Central Asian countries. This is because the ocean routes are long and prone to interdiction by other countries. This is the entire rationale for the China Pakistan Economic Corridor (CPEC) which aims to carry goods via Gwadar Port in Pakistan to western China. In addition, given the precarious economic condition of Pakistan, the success of this project is quite doubtful since the route passes through some very precarious terrain in the northern parts of Pakistan. In addition, there have been attacks on Pakistani and Chinese engineers working on some of these projects by Baloch separatists.

However, it seems that in doing so, it may be overstretching itself in what is known as "imperial overreach". We have seen that in the case of Japan during the Second World War where they secured a string of victories in Southeast Asia including in Myanmar and then came to Northeast India, where they finally lost to the Allied Forces. This was also seen in the case of Hitler during World War II when he decided to attack the then Soviet Union. The same could also be seen in the Soviet invasion of Afghanistan, which was ultimately one of the reasons for the dissolution of the former Soviet Union. There are many problems within China which need to be resolved before it goes into such massive infrastructure projects.

At the moment, we can see the BRI has run into a lot of problems in many parts of the world. The people in many countries like Pakistan (which are seen as pro-China) have been fiercely against many of the projects which are a part of the BRI and in some cases, there have been violent attacks on Chinese workers who have been a part of such projects in countries like Pakistan. The root cause is the same — which is disgruntlement at being left out of the planning process when it comes to these massive infrastructure projects and whether these projects are really needed. In addition, some governments across the world have taken huge sums of money from China as loans and this has led to instability in their own countries.

Does China Have the Domestic Wherewithal?

What is important to analyse here is whether China has the domestic wherewithal to undertake such bold ventures.

Since the BRI was first launched in 2013, the world has changed a lot and the spread of the coronavirus pandemic has changed the world a lot. The Chinese economy has been under severe stress and it is doubtful if Beijing can support such big-ticket projects anymore.

What has happened is that countries, especially those allied or close to the US, have slowly but surely moved away from China and moved on to other countries and this augurs poorly for the Chinese economy. In addition, after coronavirus pandemic, the buying power of people or what is known as purchasing power has gone down, whether in China or in other parts of the world and hence people are not making big-ticket purchases.

China has always traded with the world since the times of the famous European traveller Marco Polo and what President Xi Jinping may be trying to achieve is a revival of the Chinese Dream. To continue this big project in the future, China would need large sums of money and this does not seem likely in the near future, especially given the huge economic trouble in the country. In addition, many of the countries involved in these projects do not require these huge kinds of infrastructure projects and end up laden with debt.

Italy has already withdrawn from the BRI and this puts the onus on China as far as the BRI is concerned. It seems that as of now, it is very difficult to see how the plan proceeds in Europe. This will also impact China's other projects as Italy was supposed to be a conduit for many of the major initiatives in Europe with nations which are a part of the BRI.

In addition, a series of top-level officers in China have gone missing and this is reflective of the changes in China that are currently going on. No wonder China had a big plan for the BRI in the days when it started.

However, as things stand now, it seems that China may not be able to push the BRI-related projects through and certainly not at the speed at which it would have liked to do so earlier. The easy disbursal of loans has also been questioned since it is very different from the model which is followed by lending agencies like the IMF and the Japan-backed ADB.

China's Bigger Game Plan for the BRI

The BRI means that the neighbouring countries of China will be caught up in a kind of Chinese web since all the roads and the railway networks lead to China. Besides, another point to note here is that these countries which are a part of the BRI do not have much to sell back to China and hence the trade is mostly a one-way trade.

In addition, in most of the countries which have become a part of the BRI, they have found difficulties in paying back the loans which have been offered at very easy rates. For countries like Russia too, the BRI is a danger since they have been selling their natural resources to countries like China and natural resources are irreplaceable. For countries like Mongolia, this is a danger since pipelines like the "Power of Siberia" pipeline are planned to pass through Mongolia. What is it that Mongolia gains apart from royalty? Not much and hence this is the danger that awaits countries which are part of the BRI. While the friendship between Russia and China has grown incrementally, this has mostly favoured China and not Russia. In addition, when it comes to the trade between Russia and China, the trade is completely lopsided in favour of China.

China has always seen itself as the Middle Kingdom and this kind of mentality is at the back of this massive project: the BRI. In addition, Chinese companies have been performing at overcapacity and hence one of the main problems for the Chinese state is to dump these products in overseas markets.

For the Pushback to China's BRI

There has already been a pushback from many countries involved in the BRI. For example, in Southeast Asia, Malaysia has pushed back. China's

BRI already seems to have run into a lot of problems and there seems to be no easy out of it.

Let us analyse the reasons behind the pushback.

For example, in Myanmar, the pushback has happened because of massive projects like the Myitsone Dam. In many cases, environmental issues have been given the go-bye when approving projects for the BRI. This is because it is the host country which suffers and not China. This has led to a massive uproar and the Myanmar government had to rescind the project.

Moreover, in light of the falling property market, the Chinese authorities are going to be short of opportunities. This presents a grand opportunity for countries like India, Japan and the US to come up with some innovative solutions in the field of infrastructure development.

In addition, other countries like France are also interested in the Indo-Pacific and there could be a collaboration with them as well. It is important to note here that connectivity initiatives provide a great opportunity for countries to come closer. During its time as the Chair of the G20 in 2023, India played a very crucial role in getting the G20 countries closer and this could continue in the realm of infrastructure as well this time.

For Japan, it could represent a good opportunity to get its name back in the field of infrastructure where it has always been the leader. While the BRI has already received a good headstart, what is important is the quality of the infrastructure built and to ensure that the countries which are getting the infrastructure do not get into a debt cycle.

Many African countries like Ethiopia and Zambia have joined the BRI bandwagon, but some of them are struggling with a massive debt. Zambia became the first country to default on its debt during the pandemic.

Another problem is that plans have been finalised without proper consultations with various stakeholders. What China is actually eyeing is the resource-rich African countries since these countries have a lot of copper, cobalt or other minerals.

Roadblocks Ahead

If we take the first 10 years of the BRI, it can be said that it has achieved notable progress on some fronts. However, at the same time, it has witnessed pushback in many other parts of the world. For the BRI to be successful, China will have to tweak many of the projects which are a part of the BRI and it will have to involve the local governments in question.

The progress of the BRI will also depend on the domestic conditions of the countries which are a part of the BRI. After the pandemic, many of the countries are still struggling with basic economic issues. In addition, the fighting in the Middle East which started with the Israel–Hamas clashes has now engulfed the region with attacks on international shipping passing through the Red Sea. If things are not controlled, this once again has the possibility of weakening the economies of not only the countries in the region but also the wider world as a whole, putting paid to China's ambitions as well.

The future course of the BRI will also depend on what happens after Xi Jinping. He is now in his 3rd term as a leader and there are various reports which mention about his deteriorating health. In case a new leader were to come to power in China, would he have the same zeal to carry on with the BRI?

The demand for infrastructure could also fizzle out in the long term due to the decrease in population. In addition, many people are choosing to go back to the interior areas as they are tired of staying in urban spaces. Beijing will have to take all these facts into consideration.

Can the BRI Face the Backlash?

That is something that China will have to work on and bring some fresh ideas when it comes to the BRI. What the BRI also suffers from is the fact that it is a China-led and China-driven initiative and there are no equal partners.

This does not work well.

In addition, China's relations with many of the countries involved in the BRI, especially countries in Southeast Asia, have deteriorated incrementally and things are not the same as earlier in 2013 (when the BRI was launched).

Other Big Players in the Region Japan

Japan has enjoyed a very close economic engagement with the Southeast Asian nations. It all started with the Fukuda Doctrine of 1977 (laid out by the then Japanese PM Takeo Fukuda in a famous speech, where he resolved that Japan would never again become a military power) and Tokyo pumping in millions of dollars into Southeast Asia, both as ODA and also Foreign Direct Investment (FDI). Much of the Japanese ODA to the Southeast Asian nations went into the construction of roads, bridges, airports, power plants and industrial estates.

To begin with, it was not easy for Japan to re-engage with Southeast Asia as it had to contend with its tainted past from the times of the Second World War. However, much water has flown under the bridge since then and both the Southeast Asian nations and Japan have left the past behind.

Tokyo has been among the leading external sources of FDI for the Southeast Asian region. In 2023, it sent the second largest amount of FDI into the region, worth approximately US$26 billion. A major part of Japan's FDI has been directed into manufacturing and storage industries, along with the automotive sector. Many of the supply lines for Japanese firms are in the ASEAN region and Japanese companies have had a long foothold in the region.

Connectivity is a major focus area for Tokyo and it is worthwhile to note that earlier in March this year, it announced a new contribution of US$100 million to the Japan–ASEAN Integration Fund (JAIF). At the same time, a "Japan–ASEAN Comprehensive Connectivity Initiative" to strengthen connectivity in both tangible and intangible fronts has been launched.

Japan also has initiatives like the Partnership for Quality Infrastructure (PQI). During his visit to India, in March 2023, Japanese PM Fumio Kishida promised billions of dollars in investment to help countries across the Indo-Pacific region. This dovetails well with the Free and Open Indo-Pacific (FOIP) vision of Japan, which was launched during the times of the former Japanese PM, Shinzo Abe.

Tokyo has provided funding for many infrastructure projects in Southeast Asia. Some of the noteworthy ones include projects like the North-South Commuter Railway in the Philippines, the Bangkok–Chiang Mai high-speed rail (HSR), the Jakarta-Surabaya railway and highways, bridges, airports and ports in countries like Vietnam.

Another area where Japan leads when compared to other countries is in future-oriented projects where it provides technical and financial know-how to Southeast Asian nations to acquire and develop environment-friendly technologies. This includes projects such as the Just Energy Transition Partnership which supports energy transition in Vietnam and Indonesia, as well as the Japan–US–Mekong Power Partnership (JUMPP) for Thailand.

Challenges for Japan

When it comes to investments in Southeast Asia, there are many challenges too for Japan.

One of them is the fact that all the Southeast Asian nations have signed on to the China-led BRI and through the same, China has already deep made inroads into countries like Laos. At the same time, Indonesia has selected Chinese firms for the Jakarta–Bandung HSR Project. This is not only Indonesia's first HSR but the first one of its kind in Southeast Asia. It connects the capital city Jakarta and West Java's provincial capital Bandung and started its commercial operations in October last year.

In addition, some countries within the ASEAN like Cambodia seem to have come under the Chinese sphere of influence. At the same time, Myanmar is under civil war at the moment and there is no way that there could be fresh investments from Japanese companies in Myanmar. Meanwhile, Japanese companies which are already in Myanmar also face a very uncertain future in the times ahead.

Since the time of the Trump Administration, the relations between China and the US have gone downhill and this has worsened after the outbreak of the coronavirus pandemic. As Japan is a strong US ally, Tokyo has been forced to take a stronger line vis-à-vis China and hence it is very likely that its ties with China will deteriorate. During this visit of PM Kishida to the US, Japan has stepped up to being a "full global partner of the US". However, this would also mean enhanced responsibilities, both on the security and the economic front.

This will surely impact its economic ties with China and by extension to Southeast Asia as well where China is a major player. In the present times, Japan also has to contend with regional competitors like China and South Korea and intra-ASEAN players such as Thailand in the field of infrastructure in the Southeast Asian region.

Why Japan is Important for Southeast Asia?

Japan is very important for the Southeast Asian nations for a number of reasons. As mentioned earlier, Japan is one of the leading sources of FDI in Southeast Asia. The Southeast Asian countries would not like to put all their eggs in one basket. Some of them, especially countries like the

Philippines and Vietnam, have had territorial issues with China and this has impacted their economic ties as well. In the case of tensions with the Philippines, China cut down on banana imports from the Philippines after tensions in their political ties. In addition, China has also used tourism as a weapon since in many cases Chinese tourists were dissuaded from going to certain countries in the wake of tensions on the political front.

One major problem for the Southeast Asian nations is that when it comes to the BRI, the majority of the labour that has been used is Chinese and that has put a doubt in the minds of the local populace.

It has been estimated that the demand for airport and other infrastructure projects in Asia will rise to over US$26 trillion by 2030. Hence, Japanese companies stand a good chance. What also works for Japan is that government-backed agencies, including the Japan Bank of International Cooperation (JBIC) and the Japan International Cooperation Agency (JICA), always pitch in whenever Japanese businesses move in and in many cases, they clear the ground before major investments.

When it comes to the infrastructure front, both hard infrastructure and soft infrastructure, Japan has been at the forefront. In addition, there are other important key challenges, such as providing clean energy, and Japanese firms have been at the forefront of these challenges.

Japan's economic investments in Southeast Asia also helped build a bridge between Southeast Asia and Japan. Southeast Asian tourists are now coming to Japan in a big way. Besides, citizens from countries like Indonesia and Vietnam are working in many sectors in Japan.

Meanwhile, there is a significant increase in Chinese military activity in the region, with Chinese warships having docked for the first time at Cambodia's Ream Naval Base, which is undergoing a Chinese-funded upgrade. This is a big cause for worry for countries like Japan and also the United States.

It is worth noting here that the $6 billion Sino–Laos rail project has contributed to a big jump in the debt levels of Laos. As per the terms of the contract for the Sino–Laos rail project, Laos was to contribute 40% of start-up capital in cash and since it could not, it borrowed US$465 million — amounting to 5% of Laos GDP — from China's Export-Import Bank (Exim). In a similar case, Myanmar suspended the construction of the Myitsone Dam and then "compensated" for the suspension by granting further concessions to China in the $7.5 billion Kyaukpyu port town project.

China already has made massive inroads into many of the Southeast Asian countries like Myanmar, Thailand, Indonesia, etc. China's investment flows into Southeast Asia also increased to US$18.7 billion in 2022, or 7% of the region's total FDI. In addition, China has been upping the ante on Japanese companies and has held Japanese company executives hostage in many cases and this is a situation which is not likely to change in the upcoming future.

How is Japan Regaining Its Foothold in Southeast Asia?

It is worth noting here that while Southeast Asian nations rely on China for their economic security, they depend on the US for their strategic security. In the case of Japan, without Tokyo doing some heavy lifting on the security front, some of the Southeast Asian nations may have doubts about its capacity to deliver on the economic front.

Japan already seems to have taken a cue and apart from ODA; Japan is also now providing Overseas Security Assistance (OSA) which will be different from the ODA program that has funded roads, dams and other civilian infrastructure in the past. This would also mark a major departure from the past since previously international aid for military purposes had been strictly forbidden by Japanese laws.

Earlier in November last year, Japanese PM Fumio Kishida visited the Philippines and Malaysia. During this visit, he welcomed the signing of the Exchange of Notes concerning the provision of coastal surveillance radar system, which is the "first cooperation project under the OSA, and explained that Japan would continue to strengthen cooperation on defense equipment and technology, including the transfer of warning and control radars, and maritime security capacity building, including the provision of patrol vessels."

Recently, the Japanese Cabinet has okayed a decision to allow it to export next generation fighter jets which it is developing along with Italy and the UK. This marks a big leap forward for Japan as previously Article 9 of the Japanese Constitution forbade the export of arms to countries. In addition, it will allocate 2% of its GDP to its defence by 2027, which will make it the third biggest defence spender in the world.

Meanwhile, Japan's closest ally, the US, is trying its best to ensure that it stays in the game in the Indo-Pacific. In a historic first, the US successfully deployed a Mid-Range Capability (MRC) missile system to Northern Luzon, Philippines, earlier in April 2024 as part of *Exercise Salaknib 24*. This MRC system has the capability to reach the eastern parts of China. It is worth noting here that the Philippines has had major run-ins with China over their competing claims in the South China Sea region.

What Lies Ahead?

Japan's economy has successfully rebounded after the slump in the wake of the coronavirus pandemic. At the same time, tourists are visiting Japan in record numbers and although the yen is plummeting against the dollar, the Japanese stock market is booming.

Japan has an advantage in terms of trust when it comes to Southeast Asia and this is what it should build on. In addition, it has the first-mover advantage in the region. It could also team up with the QUAD members which include Australia and India, along with the US, to provide effective development strategies in Southeast Asia. These countries have already collaborated during the times of the outbreak of the pandemic.

To mark the 50th anniversary of the establishment of friendly relations between Japan and the Association of Southeast Asian Nations (ASEAN), a Commemorative Summit for the 50th Year of ASEAN–Japan Friendship and Cooperation was held in Tokyo in December last year. During this Summit, a joint declaration was issued which noted that "in terms of the co-creation of the economy and society of the future, efforts will be made toward enhancing public-private partnerships with a focus on the strengthening of connectivity, climate change measures, and support for small and medium-sized enterprises and startups."

What Japan needs to be careful about in Southeast Asia is that it has to provide a genuine alternative to the China-led BRI and therein lies the challenge. The difference that Japan could make would be cleaner, greener development alternatives as compared to China so that Southeast Asian nations can have an alternative option.

For Japan, Southeast Asia is crucial since the domestic market is shrinking every day. With a total population of roughly 685 million people, the Southeast Asian market is one that Japanese companies cannot ignore. The Japanese clothing major Uniqlo is already branching out into Southeast Asia and with good success.

As Southeast Asia faces a torrid summer, the lesson for everybody is that the environment is something that cannot be trod on for short-term benefits. Hence, the need of the hour is sustainable economic development and Japan is a global leader in the same. This is what it should offer to the Southeast Asian nations.

India

India, though relatively new in the infrastructure front (in terms of its presence), has made significant strides in the region, in a wide variety of countries.

These countries include Sri Lanka, Maldives, Myanmar, Iran and others. India has recently signed a 10-year agreement for the operation of the Shahid-Behesti terminal at the Chabahar Port in Iran. This agreement was signed between the Indian Ports Global Ltd. (IPGL) and Port and Maritime Organisation (PMO) of Iran. At the same time, New Delhi has offered a commitment to invest US$120 million to acquire equipment for port operations and also offered a credit window of US$250 million for developing infrastructure around the Chabahar Port.

Chabahar's importance is because of its location, just 72 km west of Pakistan's Gwadar Port. India had already spent close to approximately US$100 million to construct a 218 km long road from Delaram in western Afghanistan to Zaranj on the Iran–Afghan border to link up with Chabahar Port. Indo-Iranian cooperation on the port goes back to the 1990s when it was partially built to provide sea-land access to Afghanistan and Central Asia, bypassing Pakistan. The port is also critical for India's efforts to circumvent Pakistan and open up a route to landlocked Afghanistan. Though relations with Afghanistan have gone downhill after the takeover by the Taliban in August 2021, things could change once again in the future. In addition, this port is essential for India's connectivity with the Central Asian countries. The Central Asian countries are very rich in energy resources, something which is critical for India, as it is an energy-importing nation and has a huge population.

Challenges

However, there are quite a few challenges before the project sees success.

One of them is the situation in the immediate neighbourhood since Iran is involved in a series of conflicts in its immediate neighbourhood. Apart from the Israel–Hamas War (in which Iran is involved), in the recent past, Iran and Pakistan have also fired missiles at each other. Both sides have accused each other of harbouring terrorists. Iran has also supported Russia in its war against Ukraine, supplying drones to Russia and this has brought Tehran into the crosshairs of the Western world, especially countries like the US. The recent assassination of the Hamad leader (name) in Tehran further complicates the issue.

On the other hand, the US has also threatened that it would also be looking into the Chabahar deal. It is worth mentioning here that the US has taken a strong view of things in the past when it comes to the Iranians. For example, India had been importing oil from Iran earlier but now has shifted to other sources like Russia for meeting its domestic needs.

In addition, now things have changed after the death of the Iranian President and the Foreign Minister in a recent helicopter crash. The situation in Iran remains fluid as there are domestic dissonances in the country owing to a host of reasons and this could impact the smooth functioning of the Chabahar Port as well.

What Does India Stand to Gain?

Through the Chabahar Port, not only does India stand to gain a lot by way of access to Central Asia and Afghanistan, but it helps India emerge as a major player in the region as far as connectivity is concerned. It also provides countries like Iran an alternative to the China-led BRI.

In addition, India is a part of projects like the International North South Transportation Corridor Project which will allow it to reach countries like Russia, besides the Central Asian countries and in this respect, the role of the Chabahar Port will be crucial.

What is also interesting is that the Taliban government in Kabul has actually welcomed the development and has noted that it could provide alternate access to Afghanistan bypassing Pakistan. It is also to be noted that India has opened channels of communication with the Taliban regime in Afghanistan, after much reticence.

How Does it Stand against the BRI?

China has been making rapid inroads into the region around India. It has the China–Pakistan Economic Corridor (CPEC) which passes through Pakistan and Pakistan-occupied Kashmir.

New Delhi has been trying its best to claw back into the connectivity game in the region. On the east, it already has an initiative known as the India–Myanmar–Thailand (IMT) trilateral highway. In addition, India has been part of many connectivity especially the India-Middle Economic Corridor (IMEC) as it seeks to build new ground in the region.

For India, the connectivity angle is very important as it is the fastest growing major economy in the world. It is also to be noted that India is an energy-deficient economy and hence it needs to bring energy resources from across the world.

India's Reach out to Oceania: What's at Stake?

The visits by the Indian PM to Papua New Guinea and Australia in 2023 show that New Delhi is beginning to rise up to the China challenge in Oceania. While PM Modi visited Papua New Guinea for the third Summit of the Forum for India–Pacific Islands Cooperation (FIPIC) with his Papua New Guinea counterpart James Marape, he later on travelled to Australia for a bilateral summit with his Australian counterpart. This visit marks a far cry from the times when some sections in India thought that Oceania was very far away to matter to Indian foreign policy.

This was the first visit by an Indian PM to the island nation. The Prime Minister of Papua New Guinea was at the airport to welcome him and he touched PM Modi's feet in a gesture of respect. It is worth mentioning here that the Forum for India–Pacific Islands Cooperation (FIPIC) was launched during Prime Minister Modi's visit to Fiji in November 2014 and includes India and 14 of the Pacific island countries — Cook Islands, Fiji, Kiribati, Marshall Islands, Micronesia, Nauru, Niue, Palau, Papua New Guinea, Samoa, Solomon Islands, Tonga, Tuvalu and Vanuatu.

Why Were These Visits Important?

As for the FIPIC, this was the third summit of the series — the first of which was held in Fiji in 2014 while the second was held in Jaipur in 2015. Many of these island countries have large Exclusive Economic Zone (EEZ) and India's growing engagement with the FIPIC countries marks a serious effort to expand India's engagement with countries in Oceania. This also dovetails well with India's Act-East Policy as a part of which India has been reaching out to the countries in Southeast Asia and East Asia. Besides, Australia is very important for India as they share the same Ocean — the Indian Ocean. India and Australia have signed a civilian nuclear deal and Canberra is one of the world's leading producers of uranium. On the other hand, India is an influential member of the Quad (which includes Australia) and before PM Modi headed to Papua New Guinea, he attended the G7 Heads of State meeting in Hiroshima in Japan (as an invited guest along with the Australian PM and others).

What's in it for the Pacific Island Countries?

The island countries of the Pacific have increasingly become victims of aggressive actions on the part of China. Although they have traditionally been close to the US and countries like Australia, they are now looking towards emerging powers like India. New Delhi's presence has always been seen as benign and is very different from the role played by China. India was also the Chair of the G20 for 2023 and is also the fastest growing major economy and hence presents a new opportunity for these island countries of the Pacific.

The Australia Leg

After the Papua New Guinea leg of his tour, PM Modi went to Australia for a bilateral summit with the Australian PM. In fact, Modi was the only Head of State to continue with his trip to Australia (where a Quad Summit had been scheduled) after the US President pulled out of the Australia trip over debt relief talks at home. Later on, the Japanese PM Fumio Kishida also pulled out.

India and Australia have a growing relationship and these ties have been boosted by a host of factors including the presence of a dynamic Indian community in Australia. The two sides have already signed a "Mutual Logistics Support Agreement" which "allows military ships and aircraft to refuel and access maintenance facilities". For Australia too, India is an important security partner in the region. It has had repeated run-ins with China in the last couple of years. Although it had a booming economic relationship with China, in the last couple of years, that has deteriorated.

Challenges

There are quite a few challenges going ahead when it comes to India's reach out to Oceania.

The first is, of course, the role of China. In April last year, China and the Solomon Islands had signed an agreement ostensibly focused on boosting the latter's national security capacity. What is however worrying is that a clause in the agreement says that China can "make ship visits to, carry out logistical replacement in, and have stopover and transition in Solomon Islands," as well as send Chinese forces to the country to "protect the safety of Chinese personnel and major projects."

The second is India's growing relations with the United States. While the Papua New Guinea and the Australia legs of President Biden's tour were cancelled, due to domestic compulsions, he sent his deputy, Secretary of State, Anthony Blinken. During this visit, the United States and Papua New Guinea concluded a Defense Cooperation Agreement (DCA) and an Agreement Concerning Counter Illicit Transnational Maritime Activity Operations. This agreement (DCA) "represents a natural progression in United States' decades of defense cooperation with Papua New Guinea." The agreement will modernize our security relationship and replace an outdated Status of Forces. There are areas where India and the US could jointly reach out to these island nations.

Where Could Japan Fit in?

New Delhi could team up with Tokyo to provide infrastructure/ development solutions in these island countries as many of these countries are in danger of falling into a debt trap when it comes to their economic dealings with China. In addition, Japan has close relations with Australia as well.

There is no doubt that India's engagement with the countries in Oceania is increasing by leaps and bounds and this is only likely to continue in the future. However, the goodwill for New Delhi will have to be matched by its concrete actions on the ground. The proof of the pudding will be in the eating.

For Japan, this is a tricky situation. On the one hand, Japan has not taken part in the China-led BRI. However, at the same time, Japan is a close ally of the United States and hence it would be difficult for Japan to take a part in the Chabahar project without taking into confidence the United States.

Japan and India have worked together on projects in countries like Sri Lanka and hence it is important to continue the cooperation in other countries as well. China has stolen a march over Japan in the field of infrastructure although Japan had an early start. Japan has also been funding the growth of infrastructure through institutions like the Asian Development Bank (ADB). However, Japan has very strict quality control when it comes to funding infrastructure projects and this has come in the way of its funding in recent times.

The United States

The United States is still a heavyweight in the region in so far as the regional security situation is concerned and this is a big factor that cannot be ignored. Although the US is not directly involved in the infrastructure sector directly, what the US certainly provides is security while allows the developments in the region to go on smoothly. Many years ago, the US had renamed the Pacific Command as the Indo-Pacific Command and this could be seen as an indication of its shift in strategy.

What Happens if China is Allowed to Continue with the BRI?

What is most likely to happen is that many countries will be caught up in a debt trap as seen in the case of countries like Sri Lanka and there will be no moving out of it.

This is certainly not good news for the rest of the countries in the region.

Can Other Countries like India, Japan and the US Fill the Gap?

This is where countries like India, Japan and the US can fill the gap. It has been estimated that countries are suffering from an estimated gap in infrastructure deficit.

This is a gap that urgently needs to be filled up and it is here that nations like India, Japan and the US can fill up, especially given the fact that they are fellow democracies. It is also not a question of "if" now since Chinese influence is on the ascendance and this is collectively dangerous for all the democratic countries.

There is also the question of what happens if countries like India, Japan and the US are unable to fill the gap which has been created by China's BRI.

In that case, what will happen is that many more countries will fall under a debt trap which will make it very difficult for the residents of these countries as a whole.

Can China Redeem the BRI?

China will have to completely do away with the present BRI model which is unlikely to work in the near future. However, what is most important is whether China is willing to undertake such changes.

There is a lot of internal dissension in China over Xi Jinping's policies and in return, Xi Jinping has doubled down on the same. The future trend of the BRI will depend on the domestic economic situation in China because the main issue will be that of funds.

Development in China has also been very uneven and the central government has diverted resources to the different provinces. Meanwhile, the job market situation in China is very poor and the government seems to be at its wits' end trying to figure out what can be done. In addition, countries across the world have been reducing their trade with China and therefore China needs new markets and this is what China is trying to gain through the BRI.

China will surely make all kinds of efforts to redeem the BRI, but it is a question of whether it will succeed given the challenges and the ill-feeling for the BRI in countries across the world.

The debt trap model of the BRI will have to change in the times ahead and China will have to come up with a new model which gives precedence to the interests of the countries in question.

New Delhi will also have to incrementally increase its involvement in Southeast Asia. It has invested in the Sabang Port in Indonesia and this is significant given the fact that it is only a few hundred kilometres from

India's southernmost Andaman and Nicobar islands. New Delhi is also reaching out to other countries in Southeast Asia in a new like never before. It has been conducting joint military drills with a host of countries in the region, especially with countries like Singapore and Thailand.

The main battle for influence (as far as the BRI is concerned) will be in Asia — both in Southeast Asia as well as Central Asia. In case Japan, the US and India were to come up with a concerted plan to take on the BRI, they will have to come up with something which can counter Chinese influence in these parts of the world and provide them with a viable alternative.

Do Countries Need to Reassess their Involvement in the BRI?

Those countries which have been a part of the BRI will need to assess whether it has benefited them and if yes, to what extent. At the same time, they will need to re-assess what has been their net gain from the BRI. In addition, they also need to analyse whether their involvement with the BRI is more geopolitical or economic.

At the same time, they will have to check how much their populations have benefited from the projects which have been a part of the BRI. As we have seen in the case of countries like Sri Lanka, ordinary people have hardly benefited from such massive projects and it is the elite of some countries which has benefited from the same.

Hence, it is important that Japan, India and the US go to town with a plan which clearly addresses the needs of the ordinary people. What these countries need to realise clearly is that the BRI is a project, which clearly has China's national interests at its first priority.

China clearly does not have the interests of the BRI-participant countries first and this is something that the countries which are a part of the BRI should understand. The BRI is more of a geopolitical construct than an economic construct and hence these member countries need to understand the real purpose behind the BRI. As the ancient Chinese proverb goes, "there can be only one tiger on a mountain", and China wants to be that tiger.

Chapter 2

BRI and India

Why India Has Not Joined the BRI

One of the major countries not to have joined the BRI is India. The Indian government has time and again mentioned about the BRI being a Chinese national initiative. The former Indian External Affairs Minister (or Foreign Minister) Sushma Swaraj in one of her speeches took aim at what she described as constraints posed by connectivity that was not planned through a "consultative process." "Not just consultative but also one based on norms of transparency, good governance, commercial viability, fiscal responsibility and respect for sovereignty and territorial integrity," she said.[1]

It is to be noted here that India does not have much to gain by joining the BRI, which passes through Pakistan-occupied territory in the border state of Jammu and Kashmir and it impinges on the territorial integrity of India. While India is not part of the BRI, it is involved in a series of projects in the immediate neighbourhood which have immense potential to change the connectivity scenario in the region.

What India Needs to Worry About

The BRI is certainly worrying for India given that two of the projects — the railway network to Nepal and the China–Pakistan Economic Corridor

---

[1] https://www.livemint.com/Politics/688iHVEUK7M4DDNZUHPRwN/Sushma-Swaraj-voices-concern-over-Obor-terror.html.

(CPEC) — directly impact India and its national security. The risk has been increased manifold with the Maldives coming under the influence of China and the civil war in Myanmar.

The risk of India getting outmanoeuvred in its immediate neighbourhood is very high and this is why New Delhi must look at innovative options to tackle the threat from the China-led BRI. This is where Bangladesh plays such a critical role not only for India but also for other countries like Japan and the United States.

With Nepal, the danger is that since Nepal and India have open borders, Chinese goods coming to Nepal via the route built as a part of BRI can easily be sent to India and this can flood Indian markets to the detriment of India and Indian industry.

Hence, there is the need to provide more connectivity options to landlocked countries like Bhutan and Nepal, via India, which will ultimately benefit India in the long run. At present, transhipment of goods is a very difficult process when it comes to countries like India and Bangladesh. Here, it is important to learn from countries like Japan which have experience in Southeast Asia.

The Indian government will have to realize that the BRI could lead it to be encircled in its own background and this certainly does not augur well for the country.

Afghanistan

India had made large-scale investments in Afghanistan before the takeover of the country by the Taliban in August 2021. It has been involved in projects like the Zaranj–Delaram highway and the Salma Dam in Afghanistan before the Taliban took over. India had also helped in the construction of the Parliament in Afghanistan. One of the key reasons for Indian involvement in Afghanistan is that this country is the gateway to Central Asia. The only option now for India in Afghanistan is to wait and watch till the situation settles down.

India will also need to cooperate with countries like the US, China and Russia when it comes to the situation in Afghanistan. Already, it seems New Delhi has opened channels of communication with the Taliban and that is a good sign in the longer term.

In Afghanistan, New Delhi would have to work with the international community in order to succeed. The international community also has a big stake in bringing peace to the war-torn nation.

Myanmar

One major connectivity initiative of which India is a part is the trilateral highway between India, Myanmar and Thailand. In addition, there are projects like the Indian-backed Sittwe Port in Myanmar. The inauguration of the India-funded Sittwe Port in Myanmar is a major step forward in New Delhi's efforts to counter Beijing's growing influence in its immediate neighbourhood. The port was inaugurated by India's Union Minister for Ports, Shipping and Waterways, Sarbananda Sonowal, and the Deputy Prime Minister and Union Minister for Transport and Communications of Myanmar, Admiral Tin Aung San. They also received the first Indian cargo vessel which had departed from Eastern India's Kolkata port.

As per a press release from India's Ministry of Ports, Shipping and Waterways, this project "was conceptualized to provide an alternative connectivity to the Northeastern state of Mizoram with Haldia/Kolkata/ any Indian ports through the Kaladan river in Myanmar. The project envisages highway/road transport from Mizoram (in Northeast India) to Paletwa (in Myanmar), thereafter from Paletwa to Sittwe (Myanmar) by Inland Water Transport (IWT) and from Sittwe to any port in India by maritime shipping."[2]

What is the Advantage of the Sittwe Port?

The Sittwe Port will allow for the rapid transportation of goods between India's Northeast and other parts of the country. For a long time, the Northeastern region of India has languished behind other parts of the country when it comes to most development parameters. This process actually began in 1947 when the creation of East Pakistan robbed the Northeastern region of India of its access to the sea. Later on, East Pakistan became Bangladesh.

---

[2]https://pib.gov.in/PressReleasePage.aspx?PRID=1922760.

The Sittwe Port will also allow New Delhi to provide an alternative to the Chinese-led BRI (Belt and Road Initiative) in the region. Already China has gained a major foothold in Myanmar with the Kyaukpyu–Kumning pipeline which will take oil directly from the Middle East to southern China, thereby helping it to avoid the Straits of Malacca, which involves a lengthy detour.[3]

For Myanmar too, the port is very significant as it comes at a time when it is being ostracized by the international community owing to its actions against its own people. Myanmar's government is also cash-strapped and a huge chunk of government expenditure has gone towards funding the war campaign.

For Japan, this is a chance to collaborate with India in the field of infrastructure. Both Japan and India have not joined the BRI. In addition, with its partners in the G7, Japan has also come up with a new global infrastructure initiative named as the Build Back Better World (B3W), "a values-driven, high-standard, and transparent infrastructure partnership led by major democracies to help narrow the US$40+ trillion infrastructure need in the developing world". In addition, Japan and India are collaborating in the building of the West Container Terminal at Sri Lanka's Colombo Port.

Meanwhile, the increasing presence of China in Myanmar poses a threat to Japan's traditional influence in Myanmar. Unlike Japan, a democratic country, China (which is also a UNSC member) has been backing up the actions of the military junta at various international forums.

For a start, while it is appreciable that New Delhi has finished this project, it needs to work on other projects too, like the India–Myanmar–Thailand trilateral highway, which has been languishing behind schedule. In addition, work remains to be done on the Sittwe to Paletwa stretch and then on to Mizoram.

In addition, Myanmar has been extending the runway in its Coco Islands which is a grave danger for both Japan and India. Given the close ties between the Tatmadaw (the military junta) in Myanmar and Beijing, there are fears that it could be used by the Chinese to snoop on Indian, Japanese and shipping from other countries.

In addition, going forward, a lot depends on what kinds of items are traded between India and Myanmar. With the civil war in Myanmar

---

[3] https://www.csis.org/analysis/kyaukpyu-connecting-china-indian-ocean.

showing no signs of abating, there are doubts on whether the momentum can be sustained in Myanmar–India trade ties. In addition, India is also exploring the prospects of connectivity to Northeast India through ports like Chittagong and Matarbari in Bangladesh. In fact, Japan has financially backed the construction of a deep sea port in Bangladeshi's Matarbari.

The security situation is also worrying as the influx of refugees from Myanmar to Northeastern states like Mizoram and Manipur has led to local-level conflicts. At the same time, the Rohingya issue has strained ties between Bangladesh and Myanmar and New Delhi is in a very difficult spot as it needs to maintain good relations with both the countries.

The Sittwe Port is a part of the Kaladan Multi-Modal Transit Transport Project. It was in 2008 that India and Myanmar had inked a US$484 million deal for the Kaladan project to connect northeastern India to the Indian Ocean. The other segments of the Kaladan transport corridor project, such as the highways, have hit a roadblock due to the prevailing unrest in Myanmar and the Rohingya crisis.

Going forward, Myanmar is India's gateway to the ASEAN and New Delhi will have to understand that very clearly. Getting a foothold in Myanmar is important for both India's Act-East Policy and Japan's Free and Open Indo-Pacific Vision.

The recent developments in Myanmar have left India in a quandary as it is New Delhi's next-door neighbour and its gateway to Southeast Asia. Both the countries were under British rule and inherited similar systems of governance before they went their own ways.

However, ever since the coup on February 1, 2021, in Myanmar, after the takeover of power by the Tatmadaw, New Delhi has been caught between the devil and the deep blue sea. The generals in Myanmar are in complete control right now and although some Western countries have come out in the open, leading Asian countries like China and Japan have refrained from pushing the junta too hard.

At the moment, the ASEAN countries are trying to cajole the military junta into easing some of the restrictions, but so far that has not happened. On the other hand, in some cases, the civilians are forming resistance forces on their own. The Myanmar junta has also been hitting the opposition forces with air force, in a dangerous escalation of the present situation.

Why is New Delhi Reluctant to Wade into the Muddy Waters in Myanmar?

First, China's influence has been on the ascendance in Myanmar. Pushing the generals too hard may be costly for New Delhi as it may actually erode New Delhi's influence in that country.

Second, India has huge investments in that country. Some major projects that New Delhi is involved in are the Kaladan Multi-Modal Transit Corridor Project and the India–Myanmar–Thailand trilateral highway. The trilateral highway project assumes more significance in light of the fact that India has not joined the China-led BRI. Myanmar is also an emerging economy and that has been one of the important drivers of the economic ties.

India's Options

As of now, it would be unwise for India to wade into the troubled waters in Myanmar and there is no denying that it would be better for it to wait and watch.

So, what are the options available to India? Not many to be frank. First, India has channels of communication open with both the junta and the National League for Democracy (NLD). Aung San Suu Kyi had studied in India and has close ties with the Indian government. More important is the fact that New Delhi needs to be careful not to burn bridges with the junta in Myanmar. In the past, Indian and Myanmarese forces had conducted joint operations against militants from Northeast India holed up in that country.

Second, New Delhi is directly feeling the impact of the crisis in Myanmar as some refugees from Myanmar have taken shelter in the Northeastern state of Mizoram. The Northeastern states of Arunachal Pradesh, Nagaland, Manipur and Mizoram share a long border with Myanmar and any instability in that neighbouring country will directly impact this part of India.

Third, New Delhi will have to take a long-term view of things. In the future too, the ordinary people of Myanmar would surely keep up their struggle for justice and freedom and this kind of military rule cannot continue long into the future. Hence, New Delhi needs to take an objective view of things and also keep a channel of communication open with the protestors in Myanmar. Besides, Aung San Suu Kyi has international appeal and New Delhi should keep this in mind.

By supporting the military junta without any caveats, New Delhi runs the risk of going against the grain of international opinion on the issue of Myanmar. The best option is for India to work with the ASEAN, Japan, the US and other countries to gently nudge the generals in Myanmar to move towards democracy. Any unilateral move by India could prove to be quite detrimental to its foreign policy in the region.

It surely seems to be a long haul in Myanmar. New Delhi will have to keep its eyes and ears open and that's a huge challenge. Already China has made massive inroads into India's backyard and any more inroads by China into the region will have serious consequences for New Delhi.

Myanmar is the lynchpin of India's "Act-East Policy" and is its bridge to the ASEAN region. At this time of the pandemic, when India's economy has been hit badly, India cannot afford to lose Myanmar. This realization is what should drive New Delhi's Myanmar policy.

Indian Connectivity Initiatives in Bangladesh

India and Bangladesh are also working together to increase connectivity among them. Recently, a rail line has been inaugurated between Agartala and Akhaura in Bangladesh. All these will go a long way in increasing connectivity in the region. Bangladesh is moving up fast in the economic ladder and it will be beneficial for Bangladesh to have closer economic ties with India and this could be via the Northeast. Already the Maitri Setu, a much-awaited Maitri Setu bridge between Sabroom (Tripura) and Ramgarh in Bangladesh over river Feni, has been inaugurated. This is important since it will India access to the Chittagong Port.

In addition, there are trains running between Indian states like West Bengal and Bangladesh. Besides, geopolitical considerations demand that India rope in Bangladesh into the scheme of things when it comes to connectivity since it does not look if things in Myanmar are going to get better anytime soon.

Why Bangladesh is Important for India

First, the government of Sheikh Hasina has been friendly towards India for a long time now. This friendship goes back to the past when Sheikh

Hasina was provided shelter by India in the wake of the assassination of her father, Sheikh Mujibur Rahman.

Second, Bangladesh has been suffering from Islamic terrorism and this represents a great danger not only for Bangladesh but also for India. This is because Indian states like the Northeastern states and West Bengal are very close to Bangladesh and in the past, have faced issues due to the large-scale immigration from Bangladesh.

Third, Bangladesh has been witnessing spectacular economic development in the last couple of years which works to India's advantage. It is projected that Bangladesh will move out of the Least Developed Country status in the next couple of years. A stable Bangladesh is in India's national interests and this goes without saying.

Fourth, Bangladesh is very important for India's connectivity. The Northeastern states are connected to the rest of the country by a narrow corridor which is known as the "Chicken's Neck Corridor" and this represents a strategic threat to India. So, good ties with Bangladesh are critical for India as it will allow India to override this strategic threat. We have already witnessed what happened during the Doklam crisis of 2017 when Indian and Chinese forces clashed in Bhutan.

However, now that Shiekh Hasina has been ejected from the seat of the Prime Minister, this will look different on the ground when it comes to the ties between India and Bangladesh.

India and Nepal

New Delhi also needs to up the ante in Nepal as China has rapidly been making inroads into Nepal and it is not in India's national interest. Besides, the biggest worry is that New Delhi shares an open border with Nepal and Chinese nationals could easily intrude into India. In addition, though India has helped Nepal during the catastrophic earthquake of April 2015, even then things have not worked out in India's favour.

What India needs to work on is a new series of highways in India, which will improve. In this connection, we would also need to note the BBIN (Bangladesh, Bhutan and India) road network which has not made much progress in the last couple of years as Bhutan has not ratified the same.

Chinese BRI and Nepal

The fact that New Delhi shares a long border with Nepal has significant ramifications for New Delhi's geopolitical and strategic interests. In addition, Nepalese and Indian citizens do not need visa to enter each other's countries.

Another issue for India to ponder is why China is undertaking to fund this kind of feasibility study, which is very prohibitive, in terms of costs. The actual railroad will cost even more and the main question is the commercial viability of this project. It was in late 2018 that China prepared a pre-feasibility study of the railway. The project is estimated to cost US$5.5 billion, equal to the entire annual state revenue of Nepal. While only one-third of the total length of the tracks would fall on the Nepal side, it would account for almost half of the costs due to the difficult terrain. The moot question, however, remains the true intentions of China as to this project. Chinese entities are already running the Hambantota port project in Sri Lanka on a 99-year-old lease and are also building ports in Gwadar in southern Pakistan. On the other hand, China has investments in Myanmar, a neighbouring energy-rich nation, which has provided China an overland route for energy supplies.

All this is highly worrying for New Delhi as it has the potential to increase China's manoeuvring space in India's immediate neighbourhood. In the past, New Delhi has clearly outlined its concerns about the BRI. This proposed 170 km railway will link Kerung (Gyirong) in southern Tibet to Nepal's capital Kathmandu and will enter Nepal in the Rasuwa district and ultimately the railways will be extended to India. There is a long history to this railway link as it was proposed by the Chinese leader Mao Zedong as early as 1973 to King Birendra of Nepal in Beijing. The possibility of this becoming true became easier after the completion of the Qinghai–Tibet Railway in 2006.

This future railroad is very significant for both Japan and India as they have not joined the BRI. Tokyo has poured in massive amounts of money into India's infrastructure sector. In addition, Japan will be collaborating with India to build a high-speed railway line between Mumbai and Ahmedabad. Japan and India have experience of collaborating in the infrastructure sector in Northeast India and this should hold them in good stead. They have also been cooperating in Sri Lanka where they were initially awarded the East Container Terminal at the Colombo Port and now they have been awarded the West Container Terminal at the Colombo Port after resistance to "foreign involvement" in the earlier case.

Since Nepal is a landlocked country, New Delhi will have to help it achieve connectivity as a good neighbour. It is therefore high time that India and Japan came up with an alternate model of infrastructure development for Asian countries, especially for landlocked countries like Nepal. There could also be an alternate railroad which can be proposed by India and Japan since both the countries have expertise in building railways.

The railroad could also be a dual-use one which can be dangerous for India. Already a new round of tensions has appeared on the firmament when it comes to India–China ties, far up in the Himalayas in Tawang in the frontier state of Arunachal Pradesh.

Whenever China wants to divert attention from domestic issues, it could use the railroad to increase the pressure on India. This is one thing that New Delhi should guard against. In the long run, New Delhi will have to think of some alternative options to take on the Dragon, especially in its own backyard.

Things are going to change even more in the times ahead, especially after the change of guard in Taiwan, which seems to have caught China unawares. In addition, with the upcoming elections in the US, in case former President Trump were to come back to power, things could change drastically in the field of US–China relations.

Dangers of the BRI for India

There are quite a few dangers for India too from the BRI.

One of the dangers is the threat that neighbouring countries like Maldives are posing to India's national security interests. They have joined the Chinese bandwagon. Similar is the case with countries like Nepal.

New Delhi will have to factor in how to develop the ties with these countries which are also India's neighbouring countries. When it comes to the neighbourhood, ties with Bangladesh have proceeded well and this is where New Delhi will have to push in.

All this goes to show that the going is not going to be easy for the BRI whether it be in Asia or in other parts of the world.

What can India Do?

What India can do is finish the construction projects it has taken up in different parts of the world, especially in the neighbouring countries. It also means that New Delhi will have to give more opportunities to its neighbours to link up with it for their own progress.

For India, infrastructure is important, both within and outside the country. As India is a developing country with a large population, it is critical that infrastructure needs are being met. Millions of people are moving from the hinterlands into the cities and this is putting a huge pressure on the cities. Hence, it is important to provide good infrastructure to people so that people may work in the cities and can go back to their homes in the evening.

Japan has already been a critical partner for India as far as infrastructure development is concerned and now it is time to repeat the experiment in other parts of the world. In addition, as India has not taken part in the China-led BRI, it is important for New Delhi to provide an alternative. There are certain parts of India, especially along the Northern borders, where infrastructure growth has not kept up pace with the rest of the country.

What are the Risks for India in the Infrastructure Sector?

There are quite a few risks involved here.

One of them is the fact that investments in the field of infrastructure take a long time to recover the costs. This has been the case with the Chinese investments in the BRI and this is something that India, Japan and the United States should consider.

In addition, Japan and India have different models of infrastructure building and hence it could be a challenge to entwine the two models. The US, India and Japan have different priorities at the moment and it is difficult to see how the three can merge their differing interests.

However, when it comes to the China-led BRI, there are many lessons that India can learn from China's misadventures.

One of the most important lessons for India to learn is that it will have to avoid working with the local elites in any country. In addition, India will have to do it on a lesser scale than China since that is one issue where

China trumped as it started off with projects in Asia, Africa and Europe at the same time.

In addition, the one-size-fits-all approach that China has been working on with regard to the BRI will have to be done away with because each country is unique when it comes to its developmental needs and therein lies the lesson.

In addition, New Delhi will have to make sure that it gels well with the existing infrastructure in those countries, for example, as what happened in countries where new railway gauges were introduced.

India and Maldives

The growing Chinese influence can be seen in the immediate neighbourhood of India. The Presidential elections in the Maldives in 2023 have led to the victory of a pro-China candidate, Dr Mohamed Muizzu, and the defeat of the incumbent President, Ibrahim Mohamed Solih, who was seen as friendly towards India. The elections went into a run-off (held on September 30) as none of the candidates could secure more than 50% of the votes in the first round, which was held on September 9 last year. The new President-elect Dr Mohamed Muizzu's electoral campaign had emphasized on what he alleged was a threat to the Maldives' sovereignty posed by the Indian military personnel stationed on an island, while the incumbent President has maintained that Indian troops are in Maldives for the maintenance of the military helicopters donated by India.

What is in Store for Countries like Japan?

For Japan too, there is a note of caution here. While it does not have major investments in Maldives, what is worth noting here is that the JMSDF has a base in Djibouti and any pro-China government in Maldives could be a spanner in the works as far as Japanese deployments in the region are concerned. Japan is also an export-dependent economy, besides being a net energy importer and any volatility in the sea lanes of communication could directly impact its economic stability. Besides, the US has a base in Diego Garcia and any pro-China government in Maldives could present a security threat to countries like India, the US and Japan.

Tokyo has a Free and Open Indo-Pacific (FOIP) policy and Maldives is an important part of this policy. In addition, both Japan and India have not joined the China-led BRI and hence India and Japan should be ready to provide an alternate model of infrastructure development to Maldives, as over-reliance on China during the term of former President Yameen has already led to Maldives falling into a debt trap, with almost between US$1.1 billion and $1.4 billion being owed to China. There are chances that it may go the way of Sri Lanka, which having defaulted on Chinese loans had to give a Chinese state-run enterprise a 70% stake in the Hambantota Port on a 99-year lease, besides giving 15,000 acres around the port to Chinese firms to build an economic zone.

India and Sri Lanka

The visit of Sri Lankan President Ranil Wickremesinghe to India allowed both sides to explore a wide range of commonalities. This was his first visit to India since he took office in 2023 in the wake of the tumult which led to the then President Gotabaya Rajapaksa leaving the country. This was after massive protests in the wake of the disastrous economic slump faced by the island nation, the worst in its history since its independence in 1948.

The relations between India and Sri Lanka go back deep into the past, though in recent years, a lot has changed due to the influence of China. Beijing has been involved in a host of infrastructure projects in the country. These include a port city on Colombo's seafront. Though it was planned to become a thriving business and financial hub, things have actually not turned out so. Another such Chinese-backed project is the Mattala International Airport, in the southern city of Mattala, which was been dubbed the "emptiest airport in the world."

Such massive Chinese investments have in the past allowed Beijing to have some leverage over the government of the day in Sri Lanka, especially during the term of the Rajapaksa brothers (Mahinda Rajapaksa was President between 2005 and 2015 while his younger brother Gotabaya was the President between November 2019 and July 2022). The Chinese hand was clearly evident when India and Japan were initially granted the rights to develop the East Container Terminal at the Colombo Port and later on, it was rescinded by the Sri Lankan government in early 2021. However, India and Japan were soon offered the West Container Terminal, at the same port, clearly showing that the Sri Lankan government was trying to do a delicate balancing act.

India's Role in Sri Lanka

Traditionally, India has had an important role in Sri Lanka. It had provided support to the Sri Lankan government in the fight against the dreaded LTTE (Liberation Tigers of Tamil Eelam), which had waged a war against the Sri Lankan state (the hostilities ended in May 2009 with the military defeat of the LTTE). It is worth mentioning here that former Indian Prime Minister Rajiv Gandhi had been assassinated by the LTTE rebels.

India and Sri Lanka signed the India-Sri Lanka Free Trade Agreement (ISFTA) which came into force in 2000 and has helped uplift the trade ties between the two neighbours. In the past, India has offered many lines of credit to Sri Lanka in sectors like railways, transport, connectivity, defence, solar energy and many others. In 2021, India was Sri Lanka's largest trading partner with the overall bilateral merchandise trade standing at US$5.45 billion. In addition, New Delhi is also one of the largest contributors in terms of Foreign Direct Investment (FDI) into Sri Lanka. Total cumulative FDI from India exceeded US$2.2 billion as per the Central Bank of Sri Lanka. The major chunk of this investment from India went into areas like petroleum retail, tourism and hotels, manufacturing, real estate and telecommunications, besides banking and financial services.

Earlier, in January 2023, New Delhi was also the first to extend a letter of support towards Sri Lanka's debt restructuring efforts that helped start off the economic relief package from the IMF, which agreed to provide a US$3 billion bailout package later. During this crisis, a total of 17 countries (which extended loans to Sri Lanka) formed an official creditors committee, co-chaired by India, Japan and France to discuss Sri Lanka's request for debt treatment. This was over and above the bilateral assistance provided by India to the island nation to the tune of US$4 billion.

In March 2023, India's Foreign Minister, Dr S Jaishankar, reaffirmed India's support to Sri Lanka amidst the economic crisis, stating that "blood is thicker than water." Then there is the Buddhist angle too when it comes to India–Sri Lanka relations. In September 2020, New Delhi provided a US$15 million grant for the promotion of bilateral Buddhist linkages and an inaugural international flight carrying Sri Lankan pilgrims to the sacred city of Kushinagar in India, after it was designated as an international airport.

The China Factor

On the other hand, the China factor is a big one in the equation, especially since in the recent decade or so Sri Lanka has eased closer to China. Sri Lanka is a part of the China-led Belt and Road Initiative (BRI). When the elder Rajapaksa, Mahinda was in power (from 2005 to 2015), he opened up Sri Lanka to huge Chinese projects, much to the chagrin of New Delhi. On the flip side, in 2017, China Merchants Port Holdings took over a majority share in Sri Lanka's Hambantota port, with a 99-year lease, after it could not pay back debt incurred to build the port. It is also worth noting here that China holds around 10% of Beijing's external debt.

However, when compared to India's help during the economic crisis faced by Sri Lanka, China seemed to be hesitant to play a leading role. Beijing offered economic assistance of US$600 million in 2020 and US$2 billion in 2021 — out of which a currency swap of US$1.5 billion could be used only if Sri Lanka maintained a minimum foreign reserve worth three months of imports. Since the pro-China former Sri Lankan President Gotabaya Rajapaksa was pushed out in mid-July 2022 and a new caretaker President (in the form of Ranil Wicrekemsinghe) was sworn in, Beijing has faced a pushback and India clawed back into the diplomatic sweepstakes as Sri Lanka's most reliable partner.

New Delhi's moves in Sri Lanka are a part of its overall efforts to counter the presence of China in India's immediate neighbourhood, whether it be in Nepal, Sri Lanka or countries like Bangladesh or Myanmar or Maldives. China has set up a string of ports in countries like Sri Lanka, Pakistan and Myanmar which could have dual-use purposes as part of a so-called "String of Pearls" strategy. Meanwhile, the China–Pakistan Economic Corridor (CPEC) will allow Beijing to overcome its so-called "Malacca Dilemma" and avoid ships going through the narrow Straits of Malacca. India has a tri-services command at the strategically important Andaman and Nicobar Islands (which lies at one end of the Strait of Malacca) and this is a chokepoint. China has been trying to bypass this by building pipelines from the port of Kyaukpyu in Myanmar to southern China but the present developments in Myanmar have put a spanner in the works, as far as China's strategies are concerned.

The Sri Lankan President also met with the Chairman of India's leading conglomerate, the Adani Group, during this trip. It is worth mentioning here that the Adani Group is executing a US$400 million renewable energy project in Mannar and Pooneryn in Sri Lanka's Northern Province which is expected to be completed by January 2025. Besides, it has also pumped US$700 million towards the development of the West Container Terminal at the port of Colombo. Sri Lanka has an ambitious goal of producing 70% of its total energy from renewable energy by 2030 and India can play an important role in this quest.

Challenges

However, there are quite a few challenges here as India and Sri Lanka have had differences in the past and these could crop up again, in case there is a change of government. Sri Lanka's close ties with China in the past had created tensions with India, especially due to the visit of Chinese naval ships. Earlier in August 2023, the Chinese "research" ship Yuan Wang 5 docked at the port in Hambantota, despite Indian and American concerns about this vessel being a Chinese "spy" ship.

The Rajapaksa brothers may decide to muddy the waters and hence India needs to be careful. In addition, the Easter Bombings of April 2019 showed that there are various factors at work in Sri Lanka. When it comes to the physical execution of these connectivity projects in Sri Lanka, New Delhi may face a lot of hurdles.

The Way Forward

The best way for India to move forward in countries like Sri Lanka would be to collaborate with other countries like Japan and the US, and this would lend financial muscle and strategic heft to these projects. Japan has what is known as the Free and Open Indo-Pacific (FOIP) Vision and in addition also has a "Partnership for Quality Infrastructure" initiative.

Connectivity is the new buzzword as countries across the world have realized that it is impossible to survive economically in the post-COVID world without the same. Besides, the Indian economy is one of the fastest growing economies and there is plenty for the Sri Lankan government to learn from India's success. Time and again, India has shown that it is the first responder whenever Sri Lanka has faced any crisis, whether it be during the time of the 2004 Indian Ocean tsunami or during the recent economic crisis. It is India's national interest to keep Sri Lanka at some distance from Beijing and this July 2023 visit by President Ranil

Wickremesinghe seems to be a good start. It also marks the beginning of a new era of connectivity between the two countries whose impact will be felt for a long time.

Needless to say, New Delhi will have to wade into the waters very carefully and needs to note that there may be domestic challenges before these projects see the light of the day. At the same time, it will be naïve to conclude that India can push China completely out of the equation in Sri Lanka with these proposed connectivity projects. China will still be in the picture and there is no denying it. As seen in Chinese President Xi Jinping skipping the G20 Heads of State meeting in New Delhi in September 2023, Beijing will spare no effort to put India on the mat both in the immediate region and beyond.

At the same time, the deals signed during this visit by the Sri Lankan President to India present New Delhi with an opportunity to show that it has an alternate model of infrastructure development that is possible. However, as they say, the proof of the pudding will be in the eating.

Dangers of the BRI for India

The aims of Chinese foreign policy and especially the importance of the BRI in the same are there for all to see. One of the core aims of the Chinese state with respect to the BRI is to increase the connectivity between the inland provinces like Xinjiang, Tibet and Yunnan and this can be understood in the light of the land-grabbing moves made by China in the region.

For example, in the case of the Galwan Valley (which was attacked by the Chinese) in the summer of 2020, the Chinese tried to gain an upper hand in the region by catching the Indians unaware. They have also indulged in land grabs from the Bhutanese side and this is also worrying for India as India has a direct land border with Bhutan.

What India can expect is that China would like to keep the border with India hot because it wants to keep the outlying reasons under its active watch. While China always highlights the economic aspects of the BRI, the strategic motives of the same are never underlined. It is a very exploitative model where the interest rates are very high and countries especially the African countries get caught in what is known as a debt trap, from which there is no easy escape.

The Key for India in the Neighbourhood

The key for India in the neighbourhood will be to carry all its neighbours together when it comes to connectivity. The Modi government, very early into its first term in 2014, had enunciated what is known as the "Neighbourhood First" policy. We have seen this manifested in various ways — whether it be the Nepal earthquake of 2015 or the spread of coronavirus when India reached out to all its neighbours and provided them all the support they needed at a time when all Indians had not been vaccinated.

In addition, India has come to the rescue of its stranded neighbours in various countries like Yemen and also in the case of the Ukraine crisis when students from the neighbouring countries were also stranded in Ukraine.

India and Bhutan

One success of India's neighbourhood policy is India's ties with Bhutan. The Himalayan Kingdom is essential for India's national security, especially because of the fact that it does not maintain relations with China. In the past, China and India have almost come to war over Chinese road construction activity at Doklam in Bhutan — leading to a protracted stalemate between the two countries.

Is Bhutan Shifting Its Stand on the Sino-Bhutan Border? Time for New Delhi to Act Tough

A 2023 statement by the Prime Minister of Bhutan has stirred a hornet's nest not only in India but also in the wider neighbourhood. The PM in an interview to a Belgian newspaper had remarked that "it is not up to Bhutan alone to solve the problem . . . . There are three of us. There is no big or small country, there are three equal countries, each counting for a third."[4]

Is it an indication that Thimphu could be willing to re-negotiate the status of the tri-junction in Doklam between India, China and Bhutan?

---

[4]BBC News, Bhutan wants a border deal with China: Will India accept? available at https://www.bbc.com/news/world-asia-india-65396384.

This could be deeply problematic for India as any Chinese control of the Doklam plateau could put at risk the security of Northeast India, which is joined to the mainland by a narrow strip of land, known as the Chicken's Neck Corridor or the Siliguri Corridor. Both India and China had come very close to clashes in 2017 when China started constructing a road deep inside Bhutanese territory in Doklam.

During that time, the Indian Ministry of External Affairs (MEA) released a statement outlining India's position on the standoff. The Indian release cited a statement released by the Foreign Ministry of Bhutan, which urged "a return to the status quo as before 16 June 2017." The statement noted that "in coordination with the [Royal Government of Bhutan], Indian personnel, who were present at general area Doka La, approached the Chinese construction party and urged them to desist from changing the status quo. These efforts continue."

What are the Options Open to India?

New Delhi does not have too many options.

In this case, New Delhi should open private channels of communication with Bhutan. The Bhutanese King was recently in India and during this visit, he made all the right noises. The Joint Statement issued on the occasion of the visit of the Bhutanese King to India notes that "to take this exemplary development partnership forward, the Indian side agreed to step up support for Bhutan's 13th Five Year Plan which was welcomed by the Bhutanese side."

However, New Delhi will have to put out its concerns in no uncertain terms. The fact that any concessions by Bhutan could also leave New Delhi vulnerable to more concessions in other areas (on its border with China) should also be made clear to Bhutan. There are now reports that the Chinese have already built some villages deep inside Bhutanese territory, although Thimphu seems to be downplaying these issues.

What Japan needs to note here is that this is a reminder that China will not stop its salami-slicing tactics. This should worry Japan especially when it comes to the Taiwan issue. China has also been claiming the Japanese-held Senkaku islands and Tokyo needs to consider additional defence mechanisms to defend its key national interests. In addition, this also means that in spite of good economic relations with countries (just like China's economic ties with India), Beijing is prepared to sacrifice them at the altar of its so-called "national interests".

The Road Ahead

New Delhi should make it clear to Thimphu that it will not brook any change in stance on the issue of Doklam. Already there has been a fair bit of negative reporting on Bhutan in the Indian media since Bhutan has imposed a sustainable development fee on Indian tourists visiting Bhutan and it is not in Bhutan's interest to worsen its ties to India.

Since the launch of Bhutan's Five-Year Plans (in 1961), India has been its principal development partner with the major share of its total external grant being borne by India. It is worthwhile to note here that during the current 12th Five-Year Plan (2018–2023) of Bhutan, India's contribution constitutes 73% of the total external grant to Bhutan.

China claims three areas in Bhutan: Pasamlung and Jakarlung in the north near Tibet, and Doklam in the west near India. The sticking point in settling the border row with Beijing for Bhutan is Doklam, a plateau which offers a commanding view of the Chumbi Valley and is very close to the Siliguri Corridor.

With Xi Jinping taking over the Presidency for a third time in China, both India and Japan need to be prepared for more aggression on the border from China. Beijing's moves vis-à-vis Thimphu seem to be similar to its moves in the South China Sea, where it has built and fortified islands to strengthen its claims over disputed waters. In Bhutan, the Chinese seem to be altering the status quo, without any visible obstruction by Bhutan.

For the BRI to be successful, a wide range of objectives must be fulfilled.

First is that it must be beneficial to the people of a country where it is being constructed or else there is no point in the construction of the same.

Second, it has to gel with existing projects in the country. For example, in some countries, the existing projects in the country are not aligned with the projects in other parts of the country.

Third, the loan terms also have to be favourable to the home country or else only China will be benefitted. China has been giving loans easily, but the problem is that during the time of return, they are creating many irritants.

Another important factor in the case of the BRI is the demographic factor as China is grappling with decreasing population.

There are many parts of China where the population is decreasing very fast and hence many ghost cities have emerged. In addition, there are ghost cities in some Southeast Asian countries like Malaysia too.

So, the original plans which were envisaged when the BRI was first planned in 2013 would need to be changed.

In addition, there are other factors on which the BRI is dependent. These include the change of governments. For example, there has been a change in governments, in the case of countries like Nepal or say Maldives, and this has changed the momentum of the progress of the BRI.

Terrorism is another challenge as seen in the context of Sri Lanka which saw the Easter attacks. The going has never been the same in Sri Lanka after that.

The Pullback from Pangong Tso: Is There a Bigger Chinese Game Plan?

The Chinese pullback from the area around the Pangong Tso lake in 2021 has dumbfounded observers both in India and outside. However, the moot point is why now and is there a bigger game plan on the part of the Dragon?

Let's try to analyze the points.

First, China is facing growing pressure on many fronts and this Ladakh front doesn't bring any immediate gains for China.

Second, it actually takes India by surprise. This could well mean that China might be planning something bigger.

Third, China may also be trying to leverage its ties with the new Biden Administration in the US through this move.

Fourth, the recent Chinese move could also be seen as part of China's "two-step forward and one-step backward policy". They may have also meant it to test India's resolve and now that they have seen it, they may reformulate their response.

Fifth, at the same time, it could also be indicative of an internal power struggle between the CCP and the PLA. Chinese President Xi Jinping has also been trying to stamp his authority over the country at large and this move in Ladakh against India could well have been a part of his bigger game plan.

Options for India

Going forward, India has to be wary of this latest move as it is just a small step forward and there are lots of other sources of tension in the bilateral ties.

First, New Delhi will have to get to the bottom of the Chinese strategy in this regard. Unless it is able to comprehend the Chinese strategy, things will not fall into place.

Second, India should understand that China is still under illegal occupation of Indian territory including in the border state of Arunachal Pradesh and it is in no mood to give up on the same.

Third, it will have to increase the pressure on China in the maritime front where China is at a weak situation. In addition, India will have to hit China hard in the economic realm. This will be a big challenge since China now has a huge balance of trade in its favour. While the banning of quite a few Chinese apps is welcome, it is no substitute for a stronger Indian response.

Learning for Japan

What does China's withdrawal from Pangong-Tso mean for Japan?

China has been pressing harder on the maritime front when it comes to the Japanese-held Senkaku islands. The lesson for Tokyo is two-pronged — one in the strategic realm and one in the economic realm. In the strategic realm, it is within the realm of possibility that China might stage some similar moves to test Japan's responses and hence Japan has to be ready with a strategy in this regard. In addition, India retaliated in the economic realm against Chinese interests and this is where Japan could take a leaf out of India's book. In addition, India's tourism sector does not depend on Chinese tourists to the extent of Japan and this is a big advantage for India.

The Road Ahead

The road ahead is certainly not going to be an easy one for New Delhi. Chinese aggression seems to be at an all-time high and the Dragon seems to be in no mood to relent. In addition, as the US is fighting a deadly battle with the coronavirus pandemic, China seems to be taking definite advantage of the situation.

While the Biden Administration has promised to take a strong line towards Beijing as had happened under the Trump Administration, it is yet to lay out a clear-cut strategy in this regard.

New Delhi will have to devise some innovative responses to the increasingly flagrant moves from China. This will involve India joining hands with other democratic countries as has happened in the case of the Quad, which includes India along with Japan, the United States and Australia.

India and Myanmar

The present goings in Myanmar are certainly worrying news for New Delhi. At a time, when Maldives has already given it some headache, the ongoing civil war in Myanmar seems to have raised a lot of hackles, both for the security and the political establishments in India.

The current situation can be traced back to 1 February 2021 when Myanmar military (also known as the Tatmadaw) started a coup against the civilian government and annulled the results of the November 2020 general election. Since then, the country has been embroiled in a state of internal conflict. Of late, the junta has been on the backfoot ever since the launch of Operation 1027 in October last year by the Three Brotherhood Alliance (TBA) which includes the Arakan Army, the Myanmar National Democratic Force and the Ta'ang National Liberation Army.

New Delhi has indicated that it will scrap the Free Movement Regime (FMR) which allowed citizens from India and Myanmar to move within 16 kilometres of their border without any need for visa and the Indian Ministry of Home Affairs (MHA) has already suspended it. In addition, New Delhi has decided to fence the entire length of the land border with Myanmar which runs into approximately 1643 km. The two countries also share a maritime border. What is worrying for India is that China has been helping Myanmar in developing infrastructure in the Coco Islands, which lie very close to India's Andaman and Nicobar group of islands.

India's development assistance to Myanmar now stands at over US\$1.75 billion. Two of the major projects which India is involved in are the Kaladan Multimodal Transit Transport Project and the Trilateral

Highway Project (connecting India to Thailand via Myanmar). In addition, New Delhi has also provided assistance in setting up institutions for higher learning and research in Myanmar. It has also provided grants for the repair and conservation of 92 earthquake-damaged pagodas in Myanmar. Besides, a Line of Credit worth US$500 million has been provided to Myanmar for undertaking various projects, like the laying of an optical fibre link between Moreh and Mandalay, and for the renovation of the Thanlyin oil refinery.

What are New Delhi's Worries?

One big worry is that New Delhi has huge investments in Myanmar, especially in the infrastructure sector. India has been trying to reach out to the ASEAN nations through Myanmar which is a land bridge for India to the region. Another worry for India is that there are various rebel groups that are active in Myanmar and even in case the junta is removed, it will be difficult for India to decide whom to talk to.

The China factor is also important for India as Beijing has ties with many of these rebel groups. Hence, this could increase the bargaining power of China in Myanmar. Already China has large-scale investments in Myanmar. In addition, China has an interest in propping up the junta as Myanmar allows China access to the Bay of Bengal and thereby bypass the Straits of Malacca, which is China's Achilles Heel. There are already oil and gas pipelines which carry energy from seaports in Myanmar to southern China's Yunnan province.

What is extremely worrying for India is the influx of refugees from Myanmar into the Northeastern state of Mizoram, along with the fact that one ethnic group in the Northeastern state of Manipur has close ties with the Chin ethnic group in Myanmar and it is worthwhile to note that Manipur has been suffering from the impact of ethnic clashes for some time now. Since the coup in Myanmar, it has been estimated that more than 30,000 Myanmarese nationals, including over 40 former legislators from the National League for Democracy (NLD), have sought shelter in the Indian border state of Mizoram.

What are Delhi's Options?

To be sure, New Delhi does not have too many options as of now. It will need to wait and watch as the fighting rages on in Myanmar but at the same time will have to keep its channels open with the various groups that are operating in Myanmar.

At the same time, it will have to increase vigil at the borders abutting Myanmar since in many cases the rebels have entered India and in some cases, Myanmar government troops have been chased into Indian territory by groups such as the Arakan Army.

In addition, New Delhi will also have to work with other countries and with organisations like ASEAN while tackling the Myanmar issue. It will also have to ensure that its investments in Myanmar do not face any danger in the long term, irrespective of whichever group(s) comes to power in Myanmar.

Chapter 3

BRI and Other Countries

The third Belt and Road Forum for International Cooperation (BRF) was held in Beijing in 2023 and it is now an opportune time to analyse how far the BRI has come in the 10 years since its inception in 2013. Though this time, the lavish opening ceremony was attended by Russian President Vladimir Putin, Hungarian Prime Minister Viktor Orban, and Serbia's President Aleksandar Vučić among others, the deliberations came to a close without the "Leader's Roundtable" and joint communiqué unlike during the previous editions, which were held in 2017 and 2019.

One important aspect of this BRI Forum was the fact that it was attended by the Russian President, who has hardly travelled outside of Russia ever since the International Criminal Court issued an arrest warrant for him earlier in March 2023. This was only his second international visit, following his visit to Kyrgyzstan before that.

The BRI Debt Trap

There are two parts of the BRI, which is also known as the One Belt One Road (OBOR). One of them is the overland Silk Road Economic Belt (SREB) and the other one being the sea-based 21st-century Maritime Silk

Road (MSR). As per conservative estimates, Beijing has poured in an estimated US$1 trillion into the BRI.

Has the BRI really taken off? For that, we have to take some case studies. In Asia, two important examples could be that of Sri Lanka and Laos.

In Sri Lanka, Beijing-backed projects include a port city on Colombo's seafront, though it has not gone the way it was planned. Another such Chinese-backed project is the Mattala International Airport, in the southern city of Mattala, often dubbed as the "emptiest airport in the world", since passengers seem to have totally dumped the airport.

The same scenario can be seen in the case of Laos. It is shocking that Laos' total public and publicly guaranteed debt reached 88% of its gross domestic product in 2021, and a huge chunk of that is owed to China.

Even in Africa, things don't seem to be very much different. China had also funded the construction of a railway in Kenya with a plan to connect it to other landlocked countries in East Africa, but it seems to have derailed. On the other hand, this has left the Kenyan government servicing loans totalling around US$4.7 billion, mainly borrowed from Chinese banks.

What Will China Do?

This means that China will try to ensnare new countries into its BRI with attractive offers. It has also recently announced a new debt restructuring deal in the case of Sri Lanka whose total foreign debt stands at almost US$41 billion. This latest agreement with China's Exim Bank covers about US$4.2 billion of the country's debt.

In other parts of the world too, the same thing has happened. So, the modus operandi seems to give away loans without asking much and then when a particular country cannot pay up, it squeezes them.

What is India's Stand?

India has resolutely opposed the BRI since part of the same passes through Indian territory illegally occupied by Pakistan. The China–Pakistan Economic Corridor (CPEC) allows China to bypass the Straits of Malacca which is seen as its "Achilles Heel". The Indian Ministry of External Affairs has noted that "we are of firm belief that connectivity initiatives must be based on universally recognized international norms, good governance, rule of law, openness, transparency and equality."[1] In addition, New Delhi has also talked about having transparency in infrastructure building, something which is not really the hallmark of China's BRI (Belt and Road Initiative). In fact, there are many things for New Delhi to worry about China's increased presence in its immediate neighbourhood.

What China Gained Through the BRI

What the Chinese seem to have gained through the BRI is influence. In Sri Lanka, for example, Chinese influence was omnipresent during the terms of the Rajapaksa brothers (during Mahinda Rajapaksa's term as President between 2005 and 2015 and during Gotabaya Rajapaksa's term as President between November 2019 and July 2022). The Chinese hand was apparent when India and Japan were initially granted the rights to develop the East Container Terminal at the Colombo Port and later on it was rolled back by the Sri Lankan government in early 2021, though they were soon offered the West Container Terminal, at the same port.

All said and done, while the BRI has come a long way ever since it was launched in 2013, it seems it is fast losing steam. The coronavirus pandemic hit the Chinese economy very hard which was exacerbated by its so-called "zero covid strategy." Beijing will have to tighten its "Belt" and this is certainly not good news for the BRI.

In addition, some of those countries which have taken loans from China will never be able to pay back. One example could be seen in the case of Maldives where it took a huge amount of loan from China for a project to link the different islands.

Another test case when it comes to the BRI is the case of Pakistan. Pakistan is a part of the BRI through what is known as the CPEC (China–Pakistan Economic Corridor), parts of which pass through Pakistan-occupied Kashmir and that is one of the core reasons why India is not a part of the Belt and Road Initiative.

As a part of the same, a road is being built through PoK (Pakistan Occupied Kashmir) to reach the port of Gwadar. China needs the port

---

[1] Ministry of External Affairs, Government of India, Official Spokesperson's response to a query on participation of India in OBOR/BRI Forum, available at https://www.mea.gov.in/media-briefings.htm?dtl/28463/Official+Spokespersons+response+to+a+query+on+partic ipation+of+India+in+OBORB RI+Forum.

of Gwadar to ensure warm water access for itself. But it has run into a host of problems and it could spell trouble for Pakistan in the years to come.

If Pakistan is unable to pay back China, there are chances that it will ask for operating rights for the Gwadar port, but that could spell trouble for India, to have a Chinese-operated port right next to its western coast.

Already the western coast was used by terrorists from Pakistan to enter and cause mayhem in Mumbai on the western coast of India in November 2008. Mumbai is also India's financial capital.

In case this leads to any economic instability in Pakistan, this could be dangerous for India too as the Army could use this opportunity to assert its authority inside the country and could push terrorists into India creating new problems for India.

Afghanistan

Afghanistan is another test case for India. At present, the Taliban is in power in Afghanistan and if the Chinese were to cut deals in Afghanistan, that would be very dangerous for India's national security interests. Hence, India needs to act now in its own national security interest.

What India could offer is co-ownership in the infrastructure development process and that is important for India's relations with the neighbours as well. India already has what is known as the "Neighbourhood First" policy, and since a peaceful neighbourhood is a *sine qua non* for India's development, New Delhi would need to invest in the neighbourhood.

Already India has been invested in the region. Here, the role of countries like Iran could be very important since Pakistan has not allowed India overland access to Indian goods in Central Asia. India has already invested in the Chabahar Port in Iran, besides a railroad to the Caspian Sea. This is also part of the International North-South Transit Corridor which is very important for India.

In addition, India is an oil-importing nation and hence its energy security is very important. Central Asia is rich in energy and given the close ties between India and Central Asia, it would be important for India's energy security in the future. The TAPI (Turkmenistan–Afghanistan–Pakistan–India) pipeline seems to be going nowhere and hence India needs to check alternate options.

Myanmar

China has been involved in many projects in Myanmar and these are not necessarily a part of the BRI. China understands that Myanmar's geography is very important for it to be able to bypass the Straits of Malacca since that is a weak point for China. It has already built pipelines which allow it to bring in oil and natural gas from the Middle East directly to the southern provinces of China, and this is really a game-changer as far as Chinese energy security is concerned. These pipelines run from the Kyuakpyu Port to Ruilin in southern China. These pipelines are very important as they allow oil and natural gas to avoid going through the Straits of Malacca, thereby helping China avoid the Malacca Dilemma.

Sri Lanka

Sri Lanka has been a victim of the BRI Debt trap. In the initial days, it took a lot of loans from China but soon thereafter it got mired in debt. The economic crisis came upon it and then there was no going back. It had to be bailed out by a consortium of countries, though there are areas like the Hambantota Port which have been taken on lease by Chinese consortiums. In the case of Sri Lanka, the situation was made worse by the kind of economic crisis which it was facing. Sri Lanka later had to be bailed out by the IMF, though the economy has not recovered completely.

The Philippines

The decision of the Philippines to walk out of the China-led Belt and Road Initiative (BRI) represents a big step forward for the country as under former President Rodrigo Duterte (2016 and 2022) it had come very close to China.

The immediate provocation for the same seems to be Chinese Coast Guard's deliberate use of "dangerous blocking manoeuvres" that caused it to collide with a Philippine resupply boat about 25 km from Second Thomas Shoal. It is worth mentioning here that the Philippines had deliberately run aground its BRP Sierra Madre warship in 1999 to underline its claims to the Second Thomas Shoal, which lies within its 200-mile exclusive economic zone.

So, what are the bigger factors at work here?

For one, not much has happened on the BRI front ever since China announced some big-ticket investments in the Philippines. Second, the Philippines has borne the brunt of China's belligerence in the maritime arena in the past as it has been seen to be a weak actor in the South China Sea region.

Third, it was in June 2022 that President Ferdinand Marcos Jr took office in the Philippines, and since then, he has put relations with the US back on track, something which had taken a hit during the Duterte years. Under Duterte, China's relations with the Philippines resembled what has been termed as "pledge trap" diplomacy, where Beijing had made promises of substantial investment in exchange for concessions in the South China Sea. Later on, Manila realized that most of the promised US$24 billion in infrastructure projects never came through.

Fourth, the Philippines also seems to have learnt a lesson from the experience of countries like Sri Lanka and Laos, which seem to have been caught in a kind of debt trap as they have been unable to pay back huge loans taken from China. In addition, there are also countries like Pakistan, Kenya, Zambia and Mongolia which are now bearing the brunt of soft loans taken from China. In the case of Sri Lanka, it had to cede control of its Hambantota Port after it failed to repay Chinese loans.

What Does This Mean?

A number of Chinese projects are now expected to be put on hold in the Philippines, including the Mindanao Railway Project Tagum-Davao-Digos segment, the Chico River Pump Irrigation Project, the New Centennial Water Source Kaliwa Dam Project, the Samal Island-Davao City Connector project, and a closed-circuit television project in multiple cities throughout Metro Manila. The Philippines will also now take a re-look at the entire gamut of projects where China is involved.

Now is the right time for India and Japan to pitch in with some better initiatives in order to help nations like the Philippines. During PM Kishida's recent visit to the Philippines, he stated that both the Japanese public and private sectors would continue to support President Marcos' "Build Better More" policy, including the development of infrastructure such as the Dalton Pass East Alignment Alternative Road and the Manila

Metro Subway. During the same trip, he underlined that the relations between the two countries were "stronger than ever".

Options for the Philippines

The Philippines has the option to coordinate its response with countries like Vietnam, which have been at the receiving end of Chinese territorial aggression. Definitely, China will see this as an affront and may go all out to punish Manila in different ways. In the past, China has used economic ties as a weapon. Whenever tensions have flared up between China and the Philippines over their territorial dispute in the South China Sea, Beijing has doubled down on banana imports from the Philippines.

It was in the year 2016 that an Arbitral Tribunal constituted under the 1982 Law of the Sea Convention delivered a unanimous decision, in favour of the Philippines and firmly rejected China's expansive South China Sea maritime claims as having no basis in international law. However, the then Philippines President Rodrigo Duterte refused to press its case.

Meanwhile, the US has a Mutual Defense Treaty with the Philippines and President Joe Biden has promised to defend the Philippines in case its security were to be threatened. He noted, "I want to be clear — I want to be very clear: The United States' defence commitment to the Philippines is ironclad. The United States defence agreement with the Philippines is ironclad". Washington is bound to come to the rescue of the Philippines as a part of its Treaty Commitments under Article IV of the 1951 US-Philippines Mutual Defense Treaty.

It may be noted that China recently had concluded the third Belt and Road Forum for International Cooperation (BRF) in Beijing with pomp and gaiety in 2023, though as compared to the past few years there was much less representation at the Heads of Government level, clearly reflecting the growing lack of interest in the BRI. Meanwhile, in Europe, Italy has expressed its desire to walk out of the BRI too.

Philippines' bold move may also provide an opportunity for other ASEAN nations which are a part of the BRI to rethink the issue as they risk getting sucked into a kind of debt trap. It will also allow Manila to recalibrate its economic ties with China so that it is more balanced.

National security is paramount and no nation can afford to ignore the same, including the Philippines.

Risks Associated With the BRI

Countries which associate themselves with the BRI need to note the risks.

For one, while Chinese loans, especially those associated with the BRI, are available relatively more quickly than loans from other multilateral agencies like the World Bank or the ADB or even the IMF, the terms of these loans are often befuddled. In addition, the terms of the contract are opaque and parties are not allowed to share the same with the others, which adds to the problems.

China has some very strict conditions attached to these kinds of easy loans. For example, in the case of Sri Lanka, when it was unable to pay back the loans taken from China with respect to the Hambantota Port, it had to cede control of the areas around the Hambantota Port and also had to hand over control of the running of the port to Chinese government entities. This makes sure that countries lose their control over their own territory.

Second is that as many of the countries, especially in Africa, have found out, the Chinese bring with them their own labourers and contractors and this is very damaging to the local economy. Often these Chinese labourers and contractors are beyond the purview of the local authorities and then end up in fracas with the local authorities.

Third, the US also needs to get involved in this since otherwise China will steal the initiative from the US in the years ahead, especially in the field of infrastructure. Slowly, but surely, the US is being edged out of the game at least in the Indo-Pacific. China has also signed agreements with many of the island nations in the South Pacific, which could be a security risk for not only the US but also its allies like Japan and Australia.

Fourth, China by getting involved in the BRI is also getting hold of the local elite in most of the countries, especially in cases where the local governance is not too strong, as in the case of Africa. They then bribe the local elite and make them do their bidding, which is very dangerous for the local governments.

The connectivity gamble seems to be a big one for China. It has already invested a huge amount of money and resources into building connectivity with the ASEAN countries and quite a substantial section of the same has gone up in smoke. It will therefore be interesting to see how things develop going forward, in the field of connectivity, especially when it comes to the BRI.

Laos

One example of China's big game plan for the region is the China–Laos collaboration in the railways sector as a part of which Laos now has a high-speed railway. Now, what is important here is to understand what is needed from Laos' perspective.

Does Laos need such railways? How will it repay its debts to China?

This is yet another example of predatory financing on the part of China when it comes to countries like Laos.

Why the Chinese Want the BRI?

The BRI is a new-age avatar of the ancient Silk Road of yore which started during the Han empire but later on fell into disuse.

The Chinese want the BRI because they want to move away from the middle-income trap and in addition, they want to offload the excess capacity of Chinese manufacturing.

In addition, at the same time, China is motivated to boost global economic links to its western regions, which historically have been neglected. Promoting economic development in the western province of Xinjiang, where separatist violence has been on the upswing, is a major priority, as is securing long-term energy supplies from Central Asia and the Middle East, especially via routes the US military cannot disrupt.

With this, Chinese President Xi Jinping also wants to carve out a legacy for himself both within China and the wider world. It is also worth noting that Xi Jinping had been elected as President for a third term, thereby making him the strongest Chinese leader post Mao Zedong. It could also be a ploy to ensnare countries into a kind of debt trap as has already happened in the case of countries like Sri Lanka.

Challenges for the BRI

It is not as if there are no challenges for the BRI.

For one, the Chinese economy is faltering and it will be unable to shell out the loans permanently for a long period of time.

Second, many countries like Sri Lanka have already fallen into a kind of debt trap and new countries will be loath to join the BRI seeing the experience of countries like Sri Lanka.

In addition, the Philippines has walked out of the BRI and many countries would be following suit in the times ahead. Among Europe too, Italy has walked out.

The Risks

Hence, the risks associated with the BRI far outweigh the benefits and this is something that the countries need to learn.

This is, of course, a pet project of Xi Jinping and it seems that a certain kind of hubris has therefore set in. Hence, the question would be what would happen after Xi Jinping?

The main goal of this initiative is to make China a developed country by 2049 which is the 100th anniversary of its founding, but there are many other factors that are involved here, which include questions about demography and this is a dangerous factor as China is rapidly becoming old.

Already many cities/towns in China are becoming ghost cities, and if the current trends continue, there seem to be dangerous times ahead.

In addition, as per the projections, the population of some of the European countries, which are part of the BRI, is also expected to fall. Would there be a need for such infrastructure in the future?

As has been seen in the case of the Mattala airport in Sri Lanka (which was a part of the BRI), there is no demand. This airport has been dubbed as the loneliest airport in the world and many other signature projects of the BRI also risk falling into the same domain.

As has been seen in the case of countries like Sri Lanka, some of them have fallen into a debt trap and there seems to be no coming out of the same. The problem is that there would be no end to this. This can be seen in the case of Sri Lanka, which had to borrow money from countries like India and Japan besides international organisations like the IMF.

The Land Bridge Proposed from Thailand

Of late, Thai Prime Minister Srettha Thavisin has been pitching the idea of setting up a land bridge across the Kra Isthmus in Thailand. While this is not a new idea, it seems to have acquired renewed traction now after he took over as the Prime Minister earlier in August this year. This is, however, not a new idea. Way back in 1677, the then Thai monarch Narai the Great of the Ayutthaya Kingdom had wanted to join the two seas (the Gulf of Thailand and the Andaman Sea)

The proposed land bridge will cut down travelling time between the Gulf of Thailand and the Andaman Sea and bypass the Strait of Malacca. It would run through the Isthmus of Kra and provide an alternative to the Strait of Malacca, which accounts for 25% of the world's goods trade. However, the project is prohibitively expensive and would cost an estimated 1 trillion baht (US$27.7 billion) and involve a 90 km (55-mile) railway and road bridge between ports in Chumpon and Ranong in Thailand.

Why is the Thai PM Pitching for This?

One reason is that he is keen to get foreign investments into his country. While, of course, the project is costly and will involve a lot of planning (besides difficulties in execution), it is certainly feasible in the long term. In addition, in times when concerns about environmental pollution are growing, this land bridge will cut down on greenhouse gas emissions, since it would cut down on the total distance between the Andaman Sea and the Gulf of Thailand.

As per the Thai PM, "this will be a global mega-project, which will shorten the duration of goods transport via the channel of the Malacca Strait by six to nine days". It is worth noting here that around 70,000 to 80,000 vessels transit annually through the Straits of Malacca and it could reach its full capacity by the end of the decade. In addition, even a hypothetical closure of the Straits of Malacca is estimated to cost shipping US$65 million a week.

Besides, a land bridge across the Kra Isthmus, undoubtedly, makes for a better idea than a canal which will separate the country.

What Should be the Role of Countries like India and Japan?

Since Thailand will be unable to execute this project on its own, the Thai Prime Minister has been pitching the project abroad at various forums. The PM, who also doubles up as the country's Finance Minister, took the plan to the Belt and Road Forum in China and Saudi Arabia. Later on, he pitched the same in San Francisco on November 12 when he attended the Asia–Pacific Economic Cooperation summit.

Indian and Japanese companies, both from the private and the public sectors, should get into the act since if this major project were to get into the hands of Chinese companies, it could be disastrous for the Japanese economy. All Chinese companies are under varying degrees of government control and they could be keeping tabs on the kinds of cargo being ferried to and from Japan. In addition, they could gather intelligence on ships from not only Japan but also other like-minded countries.

Challenges

However, there are quite a few challenges going ahead:

First, one of them is the fact that goods would have to be offloaded and then reloaded at both ends and then there are issues like the political stability of Thailand, and parts of Southern Thailand have seen insurgency.

Second, in addition, the present route has served China and the East Asian countries well and there is no reason for the countries to change and invest in a new route.

Third, in addition, after coronavirus, the economies of many of the countries have taken a hit and hence they may not be in a position to invest in this kind of massive project.

Fourth, while the Panama and the Suez Canals enable ships to cut down on thousands of kilometres, by contrast, the Kra landbridge would save a transit of only approximately 1,200 km.

What Lies Ahead?

Interestingly, while China has been trying to bypass the Straits of Malacca in various ways, interest in this project seems low. This could be because the BRI (Belt and Road Initiative) has received such a hit in some of the countries that the Chinese may be loath to take such a huge risk again.

Hence, Indian, Japanese and even American firms should take a close look at this project and see whether this is feasible, both in the short as well as the long terms. Japan already has large-scale investments in Southeast Asia and this could be a good way to get back into the development sweepstakes. On the other hand, India has what is known as the "Act-East Policy" and as a part of the same, it has been actively looking at Southeast Asia. New Delhi would be developing the Sabang Port in collaboration with Indonesia, which is not very far from its Andaman and Nicobar chain of islands. Besides, New Delhi has the tri-service naval command in the Andaman and Nicobar chain of islands and any Chinese activity in its vicinity in the Kra isthmus would be detrimental to India's interests.

Thailand is keen that this should not be an only-China project and hence it presents a great chance for India, Japan and the US to invest in this once-in-a-lifetime opportunity.

Nepal

This year has seen China upping the ante in its immediate neighbourhood. While we have seen the reaction of China to Nancy Pelosi's trip to Taiwan in August 2022, what is worrying for India is that earlier this year, it was announced that China was planning a feasibility study for a new railroad right up to the border with India via Nepal.

It is also significant since India has not joined the China-led Belt and Road Initiative (BRI) while Nepal has joined the same. In addition, Indian and Chinese soldiers clashed in the Galwan Valley in the Himalayas in the summer of 2020 which led to the first casualties in fighting between the two sides in 45 years. In addition, Chinese support for Pakistan and the CPEC (China–Pakistan Economic Corridor) has been a sticking point in the ties between India and China.

At the same time, Nepal's relations with India have been fraught at some times. In addition, there have been some governments in Nepal, which have maintained close ties with China. However, more often than not, India and Nepal have had excellent relations as Nepalese soldiers even serve in the Indian Army and have been doing so for decades.

Chinese BRI and Nepal

The fact that New Delhi shares a long border with Nepal has significant ramifications for New Delhi's geopolitical and strategic interests. In addition, Nepalese and Indian citizens do not need visa to enter each other's countries.

Another issue for India to ponder is why China is undertaking to fund this kind of feasibility study, which is very prohibitive, in terms of costs. The actual railroad will cost even more and the main question is the commercial viability of this project. It was in late 2018 that China prepared a pre-feasibility study of the railway. The project is estimated to cost US$5.5 billion, equal to the entire annual state revenue of Nepal. While only one-third of the total length of the tracks would fall on the Nepal side, it would account for almost half of the costs due to the difficult terrain. The moot question, however, remains the true intentions of China as to this project. Chinese entities are already running the Hambantota Port project in Sri Lanka on a 99-year-old lease and are also building ports in Gwadar in southern Pakistan. On the other hand, China has investments in Myanmar, a neighbouring energy-rich nation, which has provided China an overland route for energy supplies.

All this is highly worrying for New Delhi as it has the potential to increase China's manoeuvering space in India's immediate neighbourhood. In the past, New Delhi has clearly outlined its concerns about the BRI. As per an Indian Ministry of External Affairs statement, "we are of firm belief that connectivity initiatives must be based on universally recognized international norms, good governance, rule of law, openness, transparency and equality. Connectivity initiatives must follow principles of financial responsibility to avoid projects that would create unsustainable debt burden for communities; balanced ecological and environmental protection and preservation standards; transparent assessment of project costs".

This proposed 170-kilometre railway will link Kerung (Gyirong) in southern Tibet to Nepal's capital Kathmandu and will enter Nepal in the Rasuwa district and ultimately the railways will be extended to India. There is a long history to this railway link as it was proposed by the Chinese leader Mao Zedong as early as 1973 to King Birendra of Nepal in Beijing. The possibility of this becoming true became easier after the completion of the Qinghai–Tibet Railway in 2006.

This future railroad is very significant for both Japan and India as they have not joined the BRI. Tokyo has poured massive amounts of money into India's infrastructure sector. In addition, Japan will be collaborating with India to build a high-speed railway line between Mumbai and Ahmedabad. Japan and India have experience of collaborating in the infrastructure sector in Northeast India and this should hold them in good stead. They have also been cooperating in Sri Lanka where they were initially awarded the East Container Terminal at the Colombo Port and now they have been awarded the West Container Terminal at the Colombo Port after resistance to "foreign involvement" in the earlier case.

Since Nepal is a landlocked country, New Delhi will have to help it achieve connectivity as a good neighbour. It is therefore high time that India and Japan came up with an alternate model of infrastructure development for Asian countries, especially for landlocked countries like Nepal. There could also be an alternate railroad which can be proposed by India and Japan since both the countries have expertise in building railways.

The railroad could also be a dual-use one which can be dangerous for India. Already a new round of tension has appeared on the firmament when it comes to India–China ties, far up in the Himalayas in Tawang in the frontier state of Arunachal Pradesh.

Whenever China wants to divert attention from domestic issues, it could use the railroad to increase the pressure on India. This is one thing that New Delhi should guard against. In the long run, New Delhi will have to think of some alternative options to take on the Dragon, especially in its own backyard.

The China–Russia Equation

The BRI has also involved Russia since Russia is now a very big partner of China. It also involves the Central Asian countries. Hence, what we need to be careful about is that China has been trying to reach out to countries which can absorb its excess production.

As Russia's relationship with the West has deteriorated, however, President Vladimir Putin has pledged to link his Eurasian vision with the BRI. Some experts are sceptical of such an alliance, which they argue would be economically asymmetrical. Russia's economy and its total trade volume are both roughly one-eighth the size of China's — a gulf that the BRI could widen in the coming years. And in the wake of the invasion of Ukraine, some analysts have said that Beijing's refusal to condemn Russia has alienated Eastern European countries that are viewed as targets of BRI.

China's Economic Slowdown and Its Impact on Japan and India

Reports are emerging from across the world which point out to the fact that China's economy now is at an inflection point. Growth rates have fallen (when compared to the last few years) and there is massive unemployment. At the same time, the real estate sector seems to be in a state of free fall and leading private sector firms like Evergrande and Country Garden are in the doldrums.

Barclays has already cut its forecast for China's 2023 gross domestic product (GDP) growth to 4.5% from 4.9%. Meanwhile, economic activity in China across sectors like retail sales, industrial output and investment failed to match expectations, thereby leading to concerns about a longer-lasting slowdown in growth.

So, What Does This Mean for China's Neighbours?

It means that President Xi Jinping might show an increasing appetite for action on the external front since on the domestic front, he is clearly on a weak footing. Earlier in August, China came out with a so-called "standard map" which includes parts of many countries and this has enraged these countries. In addition, this could mean that Japan and Taiwan could be in the crosshairs of China.

As already seen, in the aftermath of the release of treated radioactive water from the Fukushima nuclear plant by Japan into the Pacific Ocean in August 2023, Beijing created a ruckus. Among others, stones and eggs have been thrown at Japanese schools/establishments in China. This clearly proves that China will divert attention elsewhere when it comes to the economic front. There have also been attacks on Japanese citizens in China, which brings back old tensions.

In addition, this would mean that Japan would need to boost its defences. Already the Kishida Administration has significantly increased the defence budget in the light of threats from China, among others.

With India too, China seems to be in no mood to relent. It is worth mentioning here that the two countries had fatal clashes in the summer of 2020, the first in almost 45 years. In addition, Xi Jinping recently cancelled his trip to the G20 Heads of State meeting in New Delhi in September 2023 and this clearly shows that it will ratchet up the pressure on other fronts.

With the ASEAN countries too, things seem to be no better. Beijing is involved in territorial disputes with many ASEAN countries. Already we see that there is a pushback when it comes to the various actors in Southeast Asia when it comes to China's infrastructure projects.

The situation is especially worse when it comes to countries like Vietnam and the Philippines.

China's Advantages

However, on the other hand, China is investing in cutting-edge industries like semi-conductors and electric cars and these industries are likely to gain momentum in the times ahead.

Another important factor for China is that it does not have to go through an election cycle and therefore can make tough decisions. In addition, with its huge population, there is enough domestic demand when it comes to the economy. China is also a member of the RCEP (The Regional Comprehensive Economic Partnership) and hence it will be difficult to completely cut off China from the global economy.

Challenges

However, China has its own set of challenges.

These include a falling and ageing population. Though Chinese authorities have done away with the one-child policy, there are few takers for a second child. Chinese President Xi Jinping has already fired his Foreign Minister Qin Gang and two top leaders of its People's Liberation Army Rocket Force (PLARF), which handles the Chinese nuclear arsenal. This clearly shows that not all is well on the domestic front. In addition, the central government has called on the country's richest provinces — Guangdong, Jiangsu, Zhejiang, Shandong, Henan and Sichuan, which account for roughly 40% of economic output — to help the other provinces. This itself shows that not all is well.

Long-Term Impact

The long-term impact of this will be that most of the countries (except countries which are close allies of China like North Korea and Russia) will decouple from China and the Chinese economy.

Earlier, India's leading trade partner was China but now it has been replaced by the United States and this is certainly good news. Moreover, India, Japan, the US and Australia are a part of the Quad (the Quadrilateral

Security Dialogue) and these countries are also witnessing a remarkable deal of cooperation on the economic front.

While the failure of the Chinese economy is certainly news for the global economy, this is certainly not bad news. It means that there will now be two global economic orders: One would be the Sino-centric economic world order and the other one would be the non-Sinocentric world.

In March 2023, Chinese President XI Jinping was elected for an unprecedented third term as the President of China. This means that he has subsumed all powers and has become the most powerful leader after Mao Zedong.

Will China Come Out of This Slump?

It is difficult to say now if China will come out of this slump. We will have to adopt a wait-and-watch approach. Meanwhile, there have also been rumours floating around with regard to the health of the Chinese President with some reports last year talking about him suffering from cerebral aneurysm.

China could very well be a victim of its own progress. Local governments are trying to spend heavily on infrastructure building but there seem to be no takers for these projects. In addition, people are also spending less because of the pandemic years and this has brought down demand. The zero-COVID policy followed by Beijing seems to have had disastrous lessons.

Countries like India, Japan and others would do well to learn lessons from China's economic slowdown and take appropriate steps while there is time.

What China also needs to worry about is falling into what is known as the middle-income trap where it will grow old before it becomes rich. This, in itself, will be a big challenge.

Myanmar's Ongoing Construction in the Coco Islands: Why India and Japan Need to Worry

Myanmar's constructions in the Great Coco Island (part of the Coco Islands), which are very close to India's Andaman and Nicobar chain of islands, present a big challenge to India's policy planners. A report published by the London-based think-tank Chatham House shows "two new hangars, a new causeway and a residential bloc, along with a freshly lengthened 2,300-metre runway and radar station" in the Great Coco island. All these could allow military aircraft to land and the military junta (or the Tatmadaw) to spy on Indian military activity in the area. The military junta has been very proactive of late, with the bombing of villages very close to the border with India.

For some time now, these islands have been a source of great conjecture among the strategic community. Earlier in the early 1990s, it was thought that the Chinese had established a listening post on the island, though the news could never be confirmed.

These recent satellite images clearly show that Myanmar could soon be able to conduct surveillance operations from the Great Coco Island, which lies only 55 kilometres north of India's strategic Andaman and Nicobar Islands. In addition, the Indian Space Research Organization (ISRO) regularly conducts satellite and missile tests from Chandipur-on-sea and from Sriharikota, both of which are close to the Coco Islands. The bigger worry would be if Beijing were to make use of the intelligence acquired from surveillance flights from the Great Coco island in return for pumping in desperately needed cash into Myanmar's crumbling economy.

India's Andaman and Nicobar chain of islands lie at the entrance to the strategically crucial Straits of Malacca. It is estimated that every year approximately 90,000 ships pass through the narrow sea lanes of the Malacca Strait and these ships account for an estimated 40% of global trade. In addition, it is important for India's "Act-East Policy", which aims at forging closer bonds between India and the countries in Southeast Asia and East Asia. Indian PM Narendra Modi in his address at the Shangri-La Dialogue in Singapore in 2018 noted that "oceans had an important place in Indian thinking since pre-Vedic times. Thousands of years ago, the Indus Valley Civilisation as well as Indian peninsula had maritime trade. Oceans and Varuna — the Lord of all Waters — find a prominent place in the world's oldest books- the Vedas."[2]

---

[8]Ministry of External Affairs, https://www.mea.gov.in/Speeches-Statements.htm?dtl/ 29943/Prime_Ministers_Keynote_Address_at_Shangri_La_Dialogue_June_01_2018.

Why It Is Worrisome for Japan

For Japan, it is worrisome since it has a JMSDF base in Djibouti and any Chinese surveillance from the Great Coco island could put its ships at risk. In addition, Japan is an oil-importing nation and any disruptions in its oil supplies could put its energy security at risk. It is already under pressure in the wake of the Russia–Ukraine war, which has impacted Japanese investments in Russia's oil sector.

In addition, the Chinese side could also use it to threaten Japanese lines of shipping, especially in the case of hostilities over Taiwan. Of late, the sabre-rattling from China has increased particularly after the visit of the former US House of Representatives Speaker Nancy Pelosi to Taiwan in August 2022 and also in the aftermath of the recent visit of the Taiwanese President to the US earlier in March 2023.

This is also risky for Japan as these islands could become a part of China's so-called String of Pearls strategy as a part of which it is building a string of bases in the Indian Ocean like Kyaukpyu in Myanmar, Hambantota in Sri Lanka, Gwadar in Pakistan and others. These could also have dual use (both civilian as well as military) in the future.

What Are the Options Open to India?

New Delhi will have to raise its concerns with Myanmar in no uncertain terms. In case these facilities are used by China to eavesdrop on Indian military activities, it represents a serious threat.

Myanmar is already on the backfoot at various international forums due to its actions against the Rohingyas and it does not behove well for it to antagonize India, which is an influential power. Last year, India was the Chair of the G20, the grouping which includes the world's biggest economies. In addition, there are reports that once again insurgents from Northeast India are finding shelter in Myanmar. This is very worrying since the Northeast region is enjoying peace after a long time. It seems that the Generals are playing a very dangerous game and the consequences have to be pointed out to them well in advance. India is involved in a big way in the infrastructure sector in Myanmar and should use it as a bargaining chip.

Meanwhile, China has constructed a pipeline through which oil from the Middle East can be directly offloaded in Kyaukpyu in Myanmar and can be sent inland to Kunming in southern China via Myanmar. In addition, Chinese state-owned firms will be constructing a US$7.3 billion deep-water port and US$2.7 billion industrial area in a special economic zone at Kyaukpyu.

What Lies Ahead?

It is in the interests of both Japan and India and all democratic countries to ensure there is a concerted response to this cavalier attitude on the part of Myanmar. Safe and secure sea routes are *sine qua non* for the success of both India's "Act-East Policy" and Japan's "Free and Open Pacific Vision".

Chapter 4

Other Connectivity Initiatives

There are a whole lot of connectivity initiatives that are being planned across the world (which in many ways are different from the Belt and Road Initiative (BRI)).

One of them is the International North–South Transport Corridor (INSTC) — a 7,200 km (4,500 mile) long multi-mode network of ship, rail, and road route for moving freight between India, Iran, Azerbaijan, Russia, Central Asia and Europe. It involves moving freight from these nations via ship, rail and road. This corridor has become important for Russia in light of Western sanctions, which have forced it to shift trade flows from Europe to Asia and the Middle East.

For the first time, in June this year, Russia has sent two trains laden with coal to India via the INSTC, which connects Russia to India via Iran, according to Russia's national railway company.

BRI and Europe

China has been active in Europe too with its BRI. It is worth noting here that China has provided funding towards the Greek port of Piraeus, but many of the Chinese-backed projects now in Europe have been left half-done. The Chinese state-owned firm COSCO owns a 67% share in the Greek port of Piraeus. Though container volumes have increased five-fold since 2009, China has not fulfilled its contractual obligation to invest

US$300 million in port facilities, which also included expanding cruise ship facilities, new passenger terminals, hotels, warehouses and upgrading the vehicle import terminal. This calls into question Chinese involvement in Europe as part of the BRI.

Among the European nations, Hungary was among the largest global recipients of BRI investments in 2022. China, as part of the BRI, has funded new highways and a high-speed rail connection from Budapest to the Serbian capital, Belgrade, which is due to be completed in 2025, which will eventually connect to the port of Piraeus in Greece. However, on the other side, Montenegro took a US$1 billion loan from China in 2014 to build a new highway, which remains unfinished and the debt was more than a third of Montenegro's annual budget.[1]

However, it is worth noting here that Italy has already pulled out of the BRI. The Italian PM noted that the BRI has not been successful in Italy with only a fraction of the up to €20bn worth of investment in Italy promised by Beijing in 2019 having materialised. On the other hand, Italian exports to China were worth €16.4 billion in 2022, as compared to €13 billion in 2019. On the other hand, Chinese exports to Italy rose to €57.5 billion from €31.7 billion over the same period.[2]

Japan's Free and Open Indo-Pacific Initiative

This has been Japan's signature initiative back from the times of the former Japanese PM, Shinzo Abe. As part of the same, many projects have been enunciated. One of them is the growing cooperation between India and Japan in Northeast India.

Why the FOIP is important for Japan?

First, Japan, as a trading nation, depends on free and open sea lanes of traffic in the region and has benefited from the same, right from the times of the end of the Second World War. Now, China has shown a growing belligerence in the region, which could upset the scheme of things, not only for Japan but also for other sea-faring countries in the region.

---

[1] Voice of America, Ten Years Old, China's 'Belt and Road' Is Losing Allure in Europe, available at https://www.voanews.com/a/ten-years-old-china-s-belt-and-road-is-losing-allure-in-europe-/7306378.html.

[2] https://www.bbc.com/news/world-europe-67634959.

Second, the countries in Southeast Asia are very important for the success of the Japanese economy and hence the sea routes in the region must be kept open. Japan has major investments in countries like Vietnam, Thailand and others.

One of the signal initiatives of Japanese foreign policy in recent times is the Free and Open Indo-Pacific Vision. While this was conceived by the former Japanese Prime Minister, Abe Shinzo, it has been continued by successive administrations since then. As part of the same, Japan has been trying to ensure that a rules-based order is maintained in the Indo-Pacific.

Bangladesh is an important country in the Indo-Pacific region. At the same time, Japan has been investing in a big way in Bangladesh and is involved in many projects in the country. One such project is the Matarbari Port. Close to Bangladesh, Japan has invested in a big way in Northeast India. In fact, Japan is the only country which has been allowed to invest in Northeast India in a big way, given its strategic location (Northeast India shares borders with Bhutan, China, Myanmar and Bangladesh).

Japan and Bangladesh have had close ties ever since Japan recognized the People's Republic of Bangladesh on February 10, 1972, soon after its independence. Although Japan has been one of the closest development partners of Bangladesh since its birth, it has been outsmarted by China in recent times, especially after the launch of the China-led BRI, which Bangladesh has signed on to.

It was in June 2018 that the Japan International Cooperation Agency (JICA) signed loan agreements with the Government of the People's Republic of Bangladesh, to provide a loan amount of 2.655 billion yen for the development of the Matarbari Port in Bangladesh. Tokyo is also involved in the Dhaka mass rapid transport network as part of its development assistance.

Bangladesh has also moved fast in terms of its economic development. It attained lower middle-income status in 2015 and as of 2022, it is scheduled to exit the UN's list of least developed countries by 2026. The Matarbari Port in Bangladesh could also be helpful for the landlocked Himalayan countries of Nepal and Bhutan, apart from India's Northeast states, which became landlocked at the time of India's independence in 1947 and the creation of first, East Pakistan and now Bangladesh in 1971. The Matarbari Port is also close to the Sittwe Port in Myanmar and India has significant investments in the natural energy sector in Myanmar.

Why is the Matarbari Port Important for Bangladesh?

The Matarbari Port is important for Bangladesh in a host of ways. Bangladesh is one of the fastest growing countries in the Indo-Pacific but currently has two only two major ports, the Chittagong Port and the Mongla Port, and these are not enough to handle the cargo traffic. In addition, as Bangladesh is bordered by India on all sides, its seaports are crucial for the health of the country and currently carry 90% of the country's external trade. In addition, with the military coup in neighbouring Myanmar, many countries are flocking towards Bangladesh for investment opportunities. Bangladesh has also been sheltering Rohingya refugees who have been driven from their own country, Myanmar, due to ethnic violence in that country.

Is it Possible to Link Up Japanese Investments in Bangladesh and Northeast India?

Now, the moot question is whether it is possible to link up Japan's investments in Bangladesh and Northeast India.

Before that question is addressed, we need to look at some options.

First, what is the nature of goods that are going to be transported from Bangladesh to India? These could include textiles, fish products and produce from outside Bangladesh (which would be offloaded in Matarbari).

Second, what if there is a change of government in Bangladesh? The present government led by Prime Minister Sheikh Hasina is friendly towards India and Japan, but in the past, the Bangladesh Nationalist Party (BNP) government led by Begum Khaleda Zia has not been so friendly towards India. In addition, seven Japanese consultants were killed in a terrorist attack at the Holey Artisan café in a posh area of the capital city, Dhaka, back in 2016. Recently, there have been massive protests by students against the government and things don't look good.

Third, it will be challenging to link it up to Northeast India with existing roadways. Besides, the railway connectivity is poor due to a host of factors. On the other hand, India can also join hands with Japan to develop railway connectivity in Bangladesh and on its side of the border.

Prospects

Japan and India have already been cooperating in the field of infrastructure development in some countries like Sri Lanka. Tokyo is also working with Washington DC to provide an alternative to the China-led BRI, in addition to other G7 countries with the so-called Build Back Better World initiative "led by major democracies to help narrow the US$40+ trillion infrastructure need in the developing world"

At the same time, it is worth recalling here that India is now the fifth largest economy in the world while Japan is the world's third largest economy. Any cooperation in the development of the Matarbari Port and linking it up with Northeast India could be a test case for Japan–India cooperation in the field of infrastructure in other parts of the world. The two countries have already agreed to join hands in Africa with the signature initiative known as the Asia–Africa Growth Corridor (AAGC) which aims to bring together India's traditional influence in Africa and Japanese economic muscle and technological prowess. However, it will take some time before the fruits of the efforts made by Japan in the Matarbari Port in Bangladesh are realized.

The IMEC Initiative

Another connectivity initiative is the IMEC initiative. The India–Middle East–Europe Economic Corridor (IMEC) was announced on the sidelines of the G20 Heads of State Summit in New Delhi. It is a part of the Partnership for Global Infrastructure Investment (PGII), first announced in June 2021 during the G7 (Group of Seven) summit in the UK.

The IMEC would consist of two distinct corridors: an Eastern Corridor connecting India to the Gulf region and a Northern Corridor connecting the Gulf region to Europe. In his remarks at the launch of the IMEC, Indian PM Narendra Modi noted that "IMEC would help promote economic integration between India and Europe." A White House press statement on this occasion notes that "this corridor will secure regional supply chains, increase trade accessibility, improve trade facilitation, and support an increased emphasis on environmental social, and government impacts."

The signatories to the IMEC include India, the U.S., Saudi Arabia, the UAE, the European Union, Italy, France and Germany. However, as of now, it is still on the drawing board and multiple routes are being considered. In India, ports like Mundra (Gujarat), Kandla (Gujarat) and Jawaharlal Nehru Port Trust (Navi Mumbai) are being considered while in the UAE, the ports under consideration include Fujairah, Jebel Ali and Abu Dhabi. In Saudi Arabia, Dammam and Ras Al Khair ports are being considered. In Israel, the Haifa Port is being considered while in Europe the Port of Piraeus in Greece is being thought of. It is worth noting here that both the Mundra Port in India and the Haifa Port in Israel are controlled by India's Adani Group.

Advantages

First, this is a new initiative and involves big players like India and the United States. The fact that many governments in the Middle East and Europe, besides the European Union, are also on board suggests that IMEC will receive government support at all ends and this is a good sign since such massive projects will not be possible without it.

Second, as the success of the G20 Summit in New Delhi demonstrates, India has been successful in building a global consensus when it comes to issues of global development and the IMEC is another step in that direction.

Third, currently all trade between India and Europe takes place via the Suez Canal and once the IMEC becomes operational, it will definitely make it quicker. Many a time, the Suez Canal is prone to disruptions as happened when a cargo ship got stuck in the canal, which disrupted international trade.

Can Japan Be a Part of the IMEC?

Japan has what is known as the Free and Open Indo-Pacific (FOIP) initiative and also the "Partnership for Quality Initiative" and this could gel well with this IMEC. Japan has already been developing high-quality infrastructure, especially in Southeast Asia.

In the future, it could also join IMEC. As Japan is a country dependent on external trade, joining the IMEC would be in its long-term interest. This could, for example, benefit Japanese automobile companies exporting cars to Europe from plants in Southeast Asia. Already there are many new and exciting connectivity projects that are being envisioned. With global warming and melting ice, Russia and other countries may start using the Arctic route.

In addition, as the G7 countries have announced a policy of "de-risking" from China at this year's Hiroshima G7 Summit, initiatives like the IMEC will become the order of the day. The Chinese economy has been spinning out of control and it is high time all countries took into account the risk factors. In addition, countries like India have a huge trade imbalance with China and this needs to be addressed as early as possible as this cannot be allowed to continue for a long time.

Challenges

However, there are many challenges before this initiative shows results. For one, some countries which have joined the IMEC are also part of the BRI; these include Saudi Arabia, United Arab Emirates and Italy (however Italy has expressed its desire to walk out of the BRI in times to come, in the light of a change in government). These countries would be keen not to harm their growing economic ties with the world's second biggest economy: China. In fact, Saudi Arabia and the UAE have been invited to join the BRICS at the BRICS Summit in South Africa (which has China as a core member). In addition, one of the landing ports which is being considered in Europe is the Piraeus Port in Greece, controlled by the China Ocean Shipping (Group) Company — a Chinese state-owned company.

Then there is the fact that the countries involved in the IMEC are in different stages of development. In addition, some of the sections in the proposed project are yet to be completed and this could take time. Then, there are geopolitical issues of course. At present, the relations between Saudi Arabia and Israel are pretty cordial, but that has not been the case in the past. If the Haifa Port in Israel is a part of the IMEC, it could be impacted by the political situation in the region. In addition, once the IMEC takes off, countries like Egypt stand to lose a lot of revenue and we will have to see how this plays out.

However, things have become worse ever since the October 7, 2023, attack by Hamas. Since then, the region has gone into a tailspin and as it seems now, the situation has become worse, especially after the assassination of high-profile targets by the Israeli security forces.

The Road Ahead on the IMEC Front

It seems unlikely at this stage that the IMEC will be a rival to the China-led BRI. The BRI is much bigger in scope and it started in 2013, which means it is 10 years ahead of the IMEC. In addition, the BRI involves more than 150 countries and more than 30 international organizations.

However, as things stand now, the Chinese economy seems to be losing steam and this is surely to have an impact on the BRI as well. Already there are concerns in many countries which are part of the BRI that they are caught in a debt trap. This could lead to many countries walking out of the BRI in times to come.

All said and done, there is no doubt that the IMEC is an idea whose time has come.

Can India, Japan and the US Work Together in Southeast Asia?

With the end of the Cold War, India launched its "Look-East Policy" in the early 1990s and opened up its economy. It was designed to reinvigorate its ties with the Southeast Asian and East Asian countries as throughout the annals of its history, India has had deep cultural, economic and political ties with the Southeast and East Asian nations. India supported the anti-colonial movement in Southeast Asia — the convening of the Asian Relations Conference in 1947, a special conference on Indonesia in January 1949, Chairmanship of the International Control Commission on Indo-China in 1954 and the sponsoring of the Bandung Conference — all these reflected India's deep involvement in the freedom struggle being waged by the countries of the region. But the growing pro-Soviet tilt of India's foreign policy drove a wedge between India and the Southeast Asian and East Asian nations.

In the aftermath of its "Look-East Policy" (which was launched in the early 1990s), Indian economic links with the Association of Southeast Asian Nations (ASEAN) countries have seen a constant improvement. When it comes to India's physical proximity to Southeast Asia, it seldom crosses our minds that the northernmost of India's Andaman and Nicobar chain of islands lies only around 22 nautical miles from Myanmar, while the southernmost of these islands lies only around 90 nautical miles from Indonesia.

The 572 islands of India's Andaman and Nicobar archipelago are spread over an area of roughly 8,249 square kilometres and lie at the mouth of the Straits of Malacca. These straits are the second largest oil trade choke point in the world, and it is estimated that 16 million barrels of petroleum and other liquids pass through them every day.

Indeed, whether it be the Angkor Wat temple complex in Cambodia or the island of Bali in Muslim-majority Indonesia or Indonesia's state philosophy of *Pancasila*, New Delhi's ties with the ASEAN countries go back aeons ago. However, India and the ASEAN drifted away from each other in the period after New Delhi's independence from colonial rule in 1947. It was only after the opening up of the Indian economy in the early nineties and the launch of what was then called the "Look-East Policy" that things began to look up once again for India–ASEAN ties.

In the aftermath of the end of the Cold War, New Delhi had to completely overhaul its foreign policy. The "Look-East Policy", as it was then called, was launched by the government of the former Prime Minister Narasimha Rao to reach out to countries of Southeast and East Asia besides the wider Asia–Pacific region. It was subsequently continued by the former PM Narasimha Rao's successors including the National Democratic Alliance (NDA) governments.

Why is India "Acting East"?

In his address to the East Asia Summit in 2014 in Myanmar, PM Modi noted that "since entering office six months ago, my government has moved with a great sense of priority and speed to turn our 'Look East Policy' into 'Act East Policy'".[3]

So, why is this "Act-East" policy key for India?

First, for economic reasons, India must stay connected with these parts of the world which have some of the fastest growing economies in the world. PM Modi's government came to power riding on a huge wave of anger at the previous government as it was seen as being incapable of preventing India's economic decline. Hence, for PM Modi's government to succeed, it is important for India's economy to do well.

---

[3] The Hindu (2014), "'Look East' policy now turned into 'Act East' policy: Modi" available at http://www.thehindu.com/news/national/look-east-policy-now-turned-into-act-east-policy-modi/article6595186.ece. (Accessed on 10 January 2018).

Second, for strategic relations, as many of these countries lie in India's immediate neighbourhood, any instability in these countries will directly impact India. For New Delhi to succeed economically, it must have a peaceful environment and that has always been at the heart of India's foreign policy.

PM Modi's first visit outside the Indian subcontinent (during his first term in office) since taking over was to Japan where he met the former Japanese PM Shinzo Abe. During this visit, the former Japanese PM committed Tokyo to investing nearly US$35 billion in India. Soon after the inauguration of PM Modi in May 2014, the then Australian Prime Minister Tony Abbott paid a visit to India, where the two nations inked an agreement for Australia to supply uranium to India, though New Delhi is not a signatory to the Nuclear Non-Proliferation Treaty (NPT).

New Delhi has also been helped by some fortuitous turn of events in its immediate neighbourhood.

India, ASEAN and the BRI

With the term "Indo-Pacific" gaining increasing currency worldwide in both scholarly and official circles, New Delhi's foreign policy moves are being watched (and analysed) with interest across the world, especially in Asia. At the same time, countries across the world (especially in Asia) are adjusting to the rise of China. The ASEAN nations are no different. Many of them have huge amounts of trade with China while at the same time being embroiled in territorial disputes with Beijing. No wonder they are looking at increasing their foreign policy options and the rise of India has given them this option.

China's ambitious One Belt, One Road (OBOR) initiative (also known as the BRI) has taken the world by storm and forced everyone to sit up and take notice. Most Asian countries have jumped on to the OBOR bandwagon, while New Delhi opted to sit out.

At the same time, India is also reaching out to the ASEAN region in a way like never before. The India–Myanmar–Thailand (IMT) trilateral highway (which India is undertaking) has the potential to transform the economic landscape of this entire region. The IMT highway will connect Moreh in India's Manipur state to Mae Sot in Thailand via Myanmar.

So, why is this highway crucial for India?

First, it will help improve connectivity between India's remote Northeastern part and Southeast Asia. For long, the lack of physical connectivity with Southeast Asia has been an Achilles' heel in India's "Act-East Policy." The trilateral highway will improve India's connectivity with Myanmar and Thailand, and in the future, there are plans to connect it with pre-existing roads and take it all the way to Vietnam.

Second, with the construction of this road, which started as the India–Myanmar friendship road way back in 2001, the non-attendance by India at China's Belt and Road Forum in Beijing in 2014 seems to have injected a new measure of earnestness among Indian policy planners when it comes to executing such road projects.

Third, Northeast India has been lagging behind other parts of the country when it comes to infrastructure.

The OBOR initiative (also known as the Belt and Road Initiative) has been initiated by President Xi Jinping, who has often talked about the so-called *Chinese Dream*. The OBOR is in many ways a re-invention of the ancient Chinese Silk Roads which ran from China to Europe and branched off to various countries including India. Apart from the "Maritime Silk Road", the other part of the "OBOR" is the "Silk Road Economic Belt,"[4] through which China is trying to build land connectivity through the Central Asian countries to Europe.

China is a net energy importer and one of the fastest growing economies in the world. Its gargantuan appetite for energy has seen it import energy resources from various parts of the world. Beijing has slowly but steadily been trying to assert its presence in the Indian Ocean and beyond. It has also been involved in a tense standoff with the Philippines and has proceeded with the installation of missile batteries on the Woody Island in the Paracel group of islands in the South China Sea.

The former commander of the US Pacific Fleet Admiral Harry B Harris has cautioned that China was building "a great wall of sand"[5] in the South China Sea. At a speech, he noted that "expanded cooperation with India will not only be the defining partnership for the Rebalance, it will

---

[4] Xinhua(2015), Chronology of China's Belt and Road Initiative, available at http://news.xinhuanet.com/english/2015-03-28/c_134105435.htm. (Accessed on 21 September 2017).

[5] Voice of America(2015), US Admiral: China 'Creating a Great Wall of Sand' in Sea, available at http://www.voanews.com/content/us-adminral-china-creating-a-great-wall-of-sand-in-sea/2700920.html. (Accessed on 7 September 2017).

arguably be the defining partnership for America in the 21st century."[6] Meanwhile, it is worthwhile to remember that once again (as in the past) Australia, India, Japan and the US have revived the Quadrilateral Initiative, which last time (in 2007) had to be rescinded in the light of protestations from Beijing.

In addition, for the first time, China has set up a military base in Djibouti which will help China establish a foothold in a very strategic location. India has always been the resident power in the Indian Ocean region with the sole exception of the United States. Its Navy has had a commanding presence in the region between the Strait of Hormuz and the Strait of Malacca while its Andaman and Nicobar chain of islands lie at the entrance of the Strait of Malacca, which has been termed by many observers as China's Achilles Heel. The setting up of a tri-services command by India in the Andaman and Nicobar Islands gives it an unmatched reach in the region.

In many cases, India's interests in the neighbourhood are at odds with those of Beijing. For example, New Delhi has always had close ties with the island nations in the region like Sri Lanka, Maldives and Seychelles. However, of late, once again, Beijing has been rapidly trying to make inroads into what New Delhi has traditionally seen as its own "backyard".

With the term "Indo-Pacific" gaining increasing currency worldwide in both scholarly and official circles, New Delhi's foreign policy moves are being watched with interest across the world, especially in Asia. At the same time, countries across the world and especially in Asia are adjusting to the rise of China. The 10 members of the ASEAN are no different. Many of them have huge trade volumes with China while some of them are embroiled in territorial disputes with Beijing. No wonder then that they are looking at increasing their foreign policy options. The rise of India has given many ASEAN states a compelling option.

New Delhi has long had historical ties with ASEAN member countries, though it botched those ties during the Cold War days. However, ever since the opening up of the Indian economy in the early 1990s and the launch of what was then called the "Look East Policy", things have

---

[6]Admiral Harry B Harris(2016), Raisina Dialogue Remarks — "Let's Be Ambitious Together" available at http://www.pacom.mil/Media/SpeechesTestimony/tabid/6706/Article/683842/raisina-dialogue-remarks-lets-be-ambitious-together.aspx. (Accessed on 2 February 2018).

been looking up for India–ASEAN ties. After the Modi government came to power in 2014, the "Look East Policy" was re-christened as the "Act East Policy."

Since 1992, much water has flowed down the Ganges. Now there are more than 30 dialogue mechanisms between India and ASEAN, including, as the Indian Ministry of External Affairs put it, "a Summit and 7 Ministerial meetings in Foreign Affairs, Commerce, Tourism, Agriculture, Environment, Renewable Energy and Telecommunications."

Connectivity is the key issue these days for both India and ASEAN. India is constructing the India–Myanmar–Thailand (IMT) trilateral highway, which will extend all the way from Moreh in northeastern India to Mae Sot in Thailand and is expected to be completed in the coming years.

India has not participated in Beijing's BRI. Although ASEAN nations are participating in the BRI, they would like to keep their options open with regards to connectivity initiatives emanating from India and some of them are also keen on investing in infrastructure projects within India. At the same time, it needs to be stressed here that ASEAN nations do not have any territorial disputes with India and New Delhi is largely seen as a benign power in the region.[7]

Although Japan has been a major player in Southeast Asia in the field of infrastructure, it is clear that China has stolen a march over Japan in the region, especially after the launch of BRI.

First, one interesting development is that both India and Japan have not joined the BRI.

Meanwhile, India and Japan were to jointly develop the East Container Terminal at the Colombo Port in Sri Lanka. Though that specific project has been set aside, Sri Lanka approved a joint venture with India and Japan for the development of the "Western Container Terminal" in the same Colombo Port. The deal could lay down a template for cooperation between India and Japan in other parts of the world, including in Southeast Asia, in the field of infrastructure development.

Second, Japan is still one of the biggest investors in Southeast Asia in the field of infrastructure. The importance of this region for Japan can be seen in the fact that the first two countries which the former Japanese Prime Minister Yoshihide Suga visited after taking office were Vietnam

---

[7] India Biz, India records significant progress on Sustainable Development Goals, available at https://indbiz.gov.in/india-records-significant-progress-on-sustainable-development-goals/. (Accessed on 17 July 2022).

and Indonesia. This is a continuation of Tokyo's "Free and Open Indo-Pacific Vision", which was launched during the time of his predecessor, former Japanese Prime Minister Shinzo Abe.

Third, Tokyo is also trying to regain lost ground in Southeast Asia. In the past, Indonesia had selected a Chinese–Indonesian consortium over Japan to build a high-speed railway line between Jakarta and Bandung.

Japanese firms have also been increasing their investment in Southeast Asia following growing tensions between the U.S. and China over the past decade. In addition, many Japanese firms have been moving their supply chains away from China as Tokyo–Beijing ties suffer from political tensions.

Where Does India Figure?

Meanwhile, India is looking towards Southeast Asia in a big way as part of its "Act-East Policy", which aims to reinvigorate its historic ties with this region and East Asia. New Delhi has been providing loans to the Cambodia, Myanmar, Laos and Vietnam (CMLV) countries. It has extended Lines of Credit (LoC) to the Mekong region (CMLV countries and Thailand) and has disbursed approximately "$580 million for various projects which include hydro power generation, digital connectivity, rural electrification, irrigation schemes, installation of transmission lines and building of educational institutes."

It has also been investing in a big way in the infrastructure sector in Myanmar. Connectivity is a major area of collaboration with projects like the India–Myanmar–Thailand trilateral highway, which could be extended to Vietnam in the not-too-distant future. In fact, Myanmar could emerge as a major area of cooperation between India and Japan, given the close and historical ties between these two countries and Myanmar.

Another area where India and Japan are likely to cooperate in the region is in the realm of maritime security. The Indian Navy conducts a whole range of naval exercises with the navies of the region and is seen as a benign presence there. The JMSDF (Japan Maritime Self-Defense Force), too, has been increasing its cooperation with like-minded navies in the region and in some cases has also handed over assets to some of the Southeast Asian countries, which suffer from resource constraints.

Challenges

However, there is no denying that it will not be easy for India and Japan to counter China's influence in Southeast Asia.

There are many reasons for this.

First, China is the leading trade partner for many countries in this part of the world. In addition, it is also a member of the United Nations Security Council (UNSC), where it enjoys veto power. This will be key for countries like Myanmar, which have been facing international opprobrium because of its internal unrest. China has been supporting the military junta in Myanmar, even as fighting has broken out in the country between the junta and the resistance forces.

Second, both Japan and India will need to be careful when pitching joint projects in Southeast Asia, given the fact that these nations have always been keen to protect their neutral political stance. Though Japan had been advocating its "Free and Open Indo-Pacific Vision" for some time, there seems to be reluctance among some Southeast Asian nations towards the same. This is seen especially among countries like Cambodia which are veering towards China.

Third, countries in Southeast Asia had been hit hard by the second wave of the coronavirus pandemic, and hence it may take some time for the economy to recover. While it is noteworthy that the total trade between India and the ASEAN countries stood at US$86.86 billion in FY20, India has not joined the RCEP, and this could be a major drawback.

There is no doubt that both Japan and India have long-standing ties with the countries in Southeast Asia and hence it is only natural for them to be showing interest in this region once again. The Southeast Asian nations also realize that it would be unwise to put all their eggs in one basket.

Although, as of now, China is ahead in the infrastructure race in Southeast Asia, other countries are pushing back. It is here that countries like Japan and India will play a major role. The race is certainly getting hotter.

Where can Japan and India Collaborate in Southeast Asia?

First, Japan has a "Free and Open Indo-Pacific Strategy". India and Japan are also planning to cooperate in third countries and regions, which includes Southeast Asia. Ocean pollution will severely impact the economies of many of the Southeast Asian countries. The sea lanes serve to carry oil and gas to an energy-deficient Japan, and Japanese exports pass through them on their way to key markets.

Second, in addition, India has been rapidly building up metro rail technology along with countries like Japan and these could be used in Southeast Asian countries, especially in countries like Indonesia and the Philippines. There are also some planned cities in India like Chandigarh and Gandhinagar and maybe the Southeast Asian countries can take a cue from this.

Third, Japan is the world's third biggest economy and is one of the most industrialized economies and yet it is remarkably pollution free. There is a lot for Southeast Asian countries to learn from the experience of Japan in the usage of green technologies.

Fourth, the development of sustainable technologies in Southeast Asia would also depend on the usage of I-T techniques and this is where India could play a critical role. Indian IT companies already have an active presence in Southeast Asian countries and they could team up with some of the local companies to promote sustainable solutions.

In fact, Japan was a leader in providing Official Development Assistance (ODA) to Southeast Asian countries during the initial period of their growth as enshrined in the Fukuda doctrine. After the Second World War, Japan began making reparation payments to four countries, Burma (now Myanmar), the Philippines, Indonesia and Vietnam (then South Vietnam), and offering grants-in-aid to countries including Laos, Cambodia, Malaysia and Singapore.

In 1954, Japan joined the Colombo Plan, an organization formed after World War II to promote the development of countries in the Asia–Pacific region. In 1955, the Japanese Government commenced technical cooperation, hosting trainees and dispatching specialists. The targeting of Asian countries with close ties to Japan — many of which would go on to be members of ASEAN — became the basis for a long-lasting focus on Asia in later ODA activities.

Challenges

However, things are not all rosy in the equation. There a quite a few loose ends that need to be tied up. In addition, on the geopolitical front, not everything is hunky-dory since in the aftermath of the outbreak of the war between Russia and Ukraine, India and Japan seem to be sitting on opposing ends of the spectrum.

First, India, Japan and Southeast Asian countries are at different levels of development and hence coordination could be a problem. In addition, all the ASEAN nations have signed on to the BRI.

Second, eco-tourism is another area that has not lived up to its potential. Although the number of outbound tourists from India to ASEAN countries has increased, India only accounts for 3% of tourist arrivals to the ASEAN region. The number of tourists from ASEAN countries to India is nothing to brag about either.

Third, trade negotiations are at a delicate stage over the Regional Comprehensive Economic Partnership (RCEP). New Delhi has certain reservations with regard to RCEP while ASEAN nations would like India to sign on.

Fourth, the time has come for New Delhi to take some bold initiatives so that it walks the talk when it comes to its ties with Southeast Asian nations. If New Delhi loses this chance, it may repent later on. At the same time, for Southeast Asian countries, this represents a chance to avoid putting all their eggs in one basket.

The Asia–Africa Growth Corridor: What's at Stake?

The 2017 Annual Meetings of the Board of Governors of the AfDB was held in the capital city of India's Gujarat state, Gandhinagar. Though it was not the first that African Development Bank annual meeting was held outside Africa, it assumes significance in light of the announcement of the AAGC (Asia–Africa Growth Corridor) initiative and the fact that India did not send any official representation to the Belt and Road Forum held in Beijing on May 14–15, 2017. New Delhi has also supported the establishment of a regional centre of the BRICS bank or the New Development Bank in South Africa.

Why India and Japan are Interested in the AAGC?

First, there has always been a historical connection between India and Africa. As PM noted in his address at the meeting, "many communities from western India, especially Gujarat, and the eastern coast of Africa have settled in each other's lands"[8] and New Delhi would like to build on this historical contact and goodwill.

Second, India has been reaching out to Africa in a big way to Africa. It is worth noting that the third India–Africa Summit held in 2015 had representation from all 54 African countries having diplomatic relations with India. Under this government, solar energy is being promoted in a big way. New Delhi has extended 152 lines of credit to 44 African nations which are worth close to US$8 billion.[9]

Third, Japan has also been trying to get a foothold in Africa. China's BRI has left Japan with no options but to seek out alternate models and as Tokyo does not have strategic depth in Africa, it has decided to team up with India to reach out to this continent. Incidentally, Japan had sent a delegation led by Toshihiro Nikai, Secretary-General of Japan's ruling Liberal Democratic Party (LDP), to the Belt and Road Forum,[10] though Tokyo is in no hurry to join the same. Over the years, Japan's interest in Africa has progressively grown. It maintains a base in Djibouti, which is Japan's first overseas base in the post-WWII era. As seen in the deployment of the *JS Izumo*, Japan's biggest warship in the post-WWII era, under the former Japanese PM Abe, Japan is once again trying to play a pro-active role in the Indo-Pacific region

Fourth, then there are geopolitical considerations as well. Both India and Japan are trying to become permanent members of the United Nations Security Council (UNSC) and it would certainly help their case if African countries vote in favour of their bid. In addition, the location of many African countries, especially those on the Eastern seaboard, is critical for the sea lanes of communication in the region.

What's in it for Africa?

The Indian Navy has played an important role in providing security to the sea lanes of communication in the region in the face of threats and many

---

[8] http://www.pmindia.gov.in/en/news_updates/pms-address-at-the-inauguration-of-the-annual-meeting-of-the-african-development-bank/?comment=disable.

[9] http://www.mea.gov.in/Speeches-Statements.htm?dtl/28478/Prime+Ministers+Speech+at+the+inauguration+of+the+Annual+Meeting+of+the+African+Development+Bank+AfDB+Gandhinagar+May+23+2017.

[10] http://www.thehindu.com/news/international/belt-and-road-forum-triggers-china-japan-thaw/article18474732.ece.

countries in Africa look up to India as a net-security provider. Some of the African countries have had negative experiences when it comes to trade with China and hence they would surely welcome alternate models of growth and development. It was also India that was instrumental in bringing the African Union as a permanent member of the G20 at the G20 Heads of State meeting in New Delhi in September last year.

Challenges for the AAGC

It will not be easy for India and Japan to implement the Asia–Africa Growth Corridor initiative. For one, various African countries are in different stages of development. Then there are infrastructure bottlenecks. Then there is the issue of coordination between Delhi and Tokyo.

China already has an advantage when it comes to trade with Africa. The idea of the AAGC was first mooted in the joint declaration issued during the annual summit meeting between the Indian and the Japanese Prime Ministers in November 2016. They further stressed that "improving connectivity between Asia and Africa, through realising a free and open Indo-Pacific region, is vital to achieving prosperity of the entire region."[11]

PM Modi has also been trying to reach out to the Indian Diaspora across the world and his outreach towards Africa is in keeping with the same. Besides, New Delhi wants to retain its diplomatic and economic footprint in the Indian Ocean region and many of these African countries are also part of the Indian Ocean Rim Association.

As PM Modi put forth in the meeting, "India's partnership with Africa is based on a model of cooperation which is responsive to the needs of African countries. It is demand-driven and free of conditions."

Can Japan Jump on to the Connectivity Bandwagon?

There is a lot at stake for Japan in terms of connectivity. For one, Japan was the leader in the infrastructure sector in the times since the Second World War. For sure, Japan colonised much of Southeast Asia during the Second World War but made up during the period after the Second World War with what is known as the Fukuda Doctrine.

---

[11] http://mea.gov.in/bilateral-documents.htm?dtl/27599/IndiaJapan+Joint+Statement+during+the+visit+of+Prime+Minister+to+Japan.

It is worth remembering here that Japan is still the biggest investor in Southeast Asia and has a huge positive image in Southeast Asia.

The Chinese have already stolen a march over Japan when it comes to the construction of the Jakarta–Bandung High-Speed Railway and also in the case of the China–Laos highway.

This has also got to do with Japan's economy. During the time of the former Japanese PM, Shinzo Abe, Japan had already set into action the policy of moving lines of production away from China to other regions, especially Southeast Asia. The Japanese PM has visited countries in Southeast Asia and has pledged funds for the development of infrastructure in the region. This is also in line with Japan's Free and Open Indo-Pacific and what is known as the Partnership for Quality Infrastructure.

India has also accepted the Japanese Shinkansen technology and as part of the same, the Mumbai–Ahmedabad Bullet Train project is on track for completion. New Delhi has immense potential to absorb Japanese funding since it is in need of infrastructure. In addition, JICA would be funding the construction of India's biggest bridge which will connect Assam and Meghalaya. In addition, there are projects like the Delhi–Mumbai Industrial Corridor and the Chennai–Bengaluru Industrial Corridor.

On the other hand, Japan is also looking overseas for investment as demand dries down at home. Japan is already a developed country with a shrinking population and hence the demand for infrastructure is gradually shrinking at home.

Is the Thai PM's Kra Landbridge Idea Feasible?

Of late, the Thai Prime Minister, Srettha Thavisin, has been pitching the idea of setting up a land bridge across the Kra Isthmus in Thailand. While this is not a new idea, it seems to have acquired renewed traction now after he took over as the Prime Minister earlier in August this year. This is, however, not a new idea. Way back in 1677, the then Thai monarch Narai the Great of the Ayutthaya Kingdom had wanted to join the two seas (the Gulf of Thailand and the Andaman Sea).

The proposed land bridge will cut down travelling time between the Gulf of Thailand and the Andaman Sea and bypass the Strait of Malacca. It would run through the Isthmus of Kra and provide an alternative to the Strait of Malacca, which accounts for 25% of the world's goods trade.

However, the project is prohibitively expensive and would cost an estimated 1 trillion baht (US$27.7 billion) and involve a 90 km (55-mile) railway and road bridge between ports in Chumpon and Ranong in Thailand.

Why is the Thai PM Pitching for This?

One reason is that he is keen to get foreign investments into his country. While, of course, the project is costly and will involve a lot of planning (besides difficulties in execution), it is certainly feasible in the long term. In addition, in times when concerns about environmental pollution are growing, this land bridge will cut down on greenhouse gas emissions, since it would cut down on the total distance between the Andaman Sea and the Gulf of Thailand.

As per the Thai PM, "this will be a global mega-project, which will shorten the duration of goods transport via the channel of the Malacca Strait by six to nine days". It is worth noting here around 70,000 to 80,000 vessels transit annually through the Straits of Malacca and it could reach its full capacity by the end of the decade. In addition, even a hypothetical closure of the Straits of Malacca is estimated to cost shipping US$65 million a week.

Besides, a land bridge across the Kra Isthmus, undoubtedly, makes for a better idea than a canal which will separate the country.

What Should Be the Role of India and Japan?

Since Thailand will be unable to execute this project on its own, the Thai Prime Minister has been pitching the project abroad at various forums. The PM, who also doubles up as the country's Finance Minister, took the plan to the Belt and Road Forum in China and Saudi Arabia. Later on, he pitched the same in San Francisco on November 12 last year when he attended the Asia–Pacific Economic Cooperation Summit.

Indian and Japanese companies, both from the private and the public sectors, should get into the act since if this major project were to get into the hands of Chinese companies; it could be disastrous for the Japanese economy. All Chinese companies are under varying degrees of government control and they could be keeping tabs on the kinds of cargo being ferried to and from Japan. In addition, they could gather intelligence on ships not only from Japan but also from other like-minded countries.

Challenges

However, there are quite a few challenges going ahead.

First, one of them is the fact that goods would have to be offloaded and then reloaded at both ends and then there are issues like the political stability of Thailand, and parts of Southern Thailand have seen insurgency.

Second, in addition, the present route has served China and the East Asian countries well and there is no reason for the countries to change and invest in a new route.

Third, in addition, after coronavirus, the economies of many of the countries have taken a hit and hence they may not be in a position to invest in this kind of massive project.

Fourth, while the Panama and the Suez Canals enable ships to cut down on thousands of kilometres, by contrast, the Kra landbridge would save a transit of only approximately 1,200 km.

What Lies Ahead?

Interestingly, while China has been trying to bypass the Straits of Malacca in various ways, interest in this project seems low. This could be because the BRI has received such a hit in some of the countries that the Chinese may be loath to take such a huge risk again.

Hence, Indian, Japanese and even American firms should take a close look at this project and see whether this is feasible, both in the short as well as the long term. Japan already has large-scale investments in Southeast Asia and this could be a good way to get back into the development sweepstakes. New Delhi would be developing the Sabang Port in collaboration with Indonesia, which is not very far from its Andaman and Nicobar chain of islands. Besides, New Delhi has the tri-service naval command in the Andaman and Nicobar chain of islands and any Chinese activity in its vicinity in the Kra Isthmus would be detrimental to India's interests.

Thailand is keen that this should not be an only-China project and hence it presents a great chance for India, Japan and the US to invest in this once-in-a-lifetime opportunity.

The Key About These Alternative Connectivity Initiatives

The key about all these alternate connectivity initiatives is that they are very disjointed and unlike the BRI, they do not have a common agenda.

India is a part of many of these alternate connectivity initiatives, whether it be the IMEC, the AAGC, etc., but what is important to note is that these are not India-specific initiatives. On the other hand, Japan is a part of only the AAGC and even this has not seen much progress, ever since it was started.

Hence, there is a need for a common initiative which can bring all these together and in this kind of an initiative; it is countries like India, Japan and the US which can take the lead. The African nations are an important part of the infrastructure story since they are lacking in the same and hence they need an alternate roadmap in place.

India is already investing in a big way in the field of port-led growth, as seen in the Sagarmala initiative. As per the Government of India website, the Sagarmala project, "the Sagarmala Programme, a flagship initiative of the Ministry of Ports, Shipping and Waterways, represents a visionary approach by the Government of India to transform the country's maritime sector. With India's extensive coastline, navigable waterways, and strategic maritime trade routes, Sagarmala aims to unlock the untapped potential of these resources for port-led development and coastal community upliftment."[12]

"Sagarmala seeks to enhance the performance of the logistics sector by reducing logistics costs for both domestic and international trade. By leveraging coastal and waterway transportation, the program aims to minimize the need for extensive infrastructure investments, thus making

---

[12] Ministry of Ports, Shipping ands Waterways, https://sagarmala.gov.in/about-sagarmala/introduction#:~:text=The%20Sagarmala%20Programme%2C%20a%20flagship, transform%20the%2 0country's%20maritime%20sector.

logistics more efficient and improving the competitiveness of Indian exports."

In addition, Indian private sector firms like the Adanis have been investing in ports across the world. This is a good sign for the Indian presence in the infrastructure sector, which has till now been minimal.

In addition, India has a huge coastline which needs to be put to use. As of now, countries like Singapore and Malaysia have much more bigger and efficient ports than India.

Chapter 5

Conclusion

In the previous chapters, we have seen how India, Japan and the US have been trying out various connectivity initiatives, albeit separately. These efforts are different from those of the China-led BRI since there is no common and unified blueprint that these nations have. However, there are quite a few challenges for these countries going forward, especially in their immediate neighbourhoods.

Let us analyse these challenges.

India's Challenges in the Neighbourhood

The results of the Presidential elections in the Maldives in 2023 seem to point towards fresh trouble for India's outreach to the neighbouring island country. These elections went into a runoff as no candidate secured 50% of the votes in the first round. The former President, Ibrahim Mohamed Solih, from the Maldivian Democratic Party, who was seen as pro-India, was defeated by his rival, Dr Mohamed Muizzu, who had fought the electoral race on an "India Out" campaign, promising to push Indian troops out of the island nation. Dr Muizzu is seen as being friendlier towards China than his immediate predecessor. While former President Solih had maintained that the Indian military presence in Maldives was only to build a dockyard and to operate two helicopters donated by India earlier, Dr Muizzi's campaign seems to have resonated with the electorate.

Maldives' physical proximity to India (it is barely 70 nautical miles away from India's Minicoy islands and 300 nautical miles away from India's west coast) makes these islands extremely important for India and also because they sit astride important sea lanes of communication in the region.

Does it Mean Endgame for New Delhi in the Maldives?

New Delhi has been in this kind of situation earlier too.

Under then President Abdullah Yameen's watch (during his tenure between 2013 and 2018) Maldives had joined China's Belt and Road Initiative (BRI) and its foreign policy took a pro-Beijing turn. During this period, Maldives borrowed heavily from China, so much so that racked up an estimated debt of between $1.1 billion and $1.4 billion. New Delhi once again saw a reversal of fortunes in 2018 in its favour when President Solih came to power. The latest election results are just one more round in this see-saw struggle for influence in the Maldives between China and India.

India has always had a pre-eminent role in Maldives. It had sent troops to counter the 1998 coup attempt and was the first responder during the 2004 Indian Ocean tsunami. New Delhi also sent help to Maldives during the water crisis of 2014 and also in the aftermath of the outbreak of the coronavirus pandemic. It also provided a soft loan of $250 million to Maldives to help it overcome the economic slump in the wake of the coronavirus pandemic.

New Delhi is involved in a big way in the infrastructure sector in Maldives. The biggest India-backed project is the Greater Male Connectivity Project (GMCP) for which it has provided a grant of $100 million and a $400 million line of credit. As part of the project, a 6.74 km long bridge and causeway link will connect the national capital Male with three adjoining islands: Villingli, Gulhifalhu and Thilafushi. This bridge will be nearly three times longer than the $200 million China–Maldives Friendship Bridge which was built under President Yameen's watch. In addition, New Delhi is also assisting 45 other projects in the country with a grant assistance of approximately $16.88 million.

Indian PM Narendra Modi congratulated the new President Muizzu and had reaffirmed that "India remains committed to strengthening the time-tested India-Maldives bilateral relationship and enhancing our over-all cooperation in the Indian Ocean Region." As regards the struggle for influence in the region with China, this is likely to continue whether it be in the Maldives or in countries like Sri Lanka, Nepal or Myanmar. Some time ago, the same kind of situation was seen in Sri Lanka when it faced economic collapse in 2019 and India was again one of the first countries to help out, though the two countries were not on the best of terms at that time.

In November 2019, Gotabaya Rajapaksa took over as President in Sri Lanka from former President Maithripala Sirisena and once again the pendulum swung China's way since the Rajapaksa brothers have the reputation of being pro-China. However, Gotabaya Rajapaksa was forced out of office in July 2022 amidst massive protests and after that, Ranil Wickremesinghe became the President, who is seen as being much more friendly towards India than the Rajapaksas.

While the new President in the Maldives could spell trouble for India in the days ahead, it will be difficult for the new President to wish away India's presence and influence in the Maldives. At the same time, New Delhi will have to look at the bigger picture which is that the recent Presidential election marks another step forward for Maldives since it held its first multi-party elections only as late as 2008. It means that democracy is taking strong roots in Maldives, which should be music to New Delhi's ears.

The catchword here for New Delhi will be patience. In cricketing terminology, India may have lost some wickets in Maldives as of now but is certainly very much in the game.

Can India, Japan and the US Work Together?

There is a big scope for countries like India, Japan and the US to work together on creating a new kind of infrastructure development which will take the infrastructure needs of countries in Asia and Europe into account.

This will also need technology since it is important to keep the local climate in mind. In many places, the BRI has not been successful since it has failed to take into account the local realities. India, Japan and the US could work on a sustainable infrastructure initiative. Japan has a lot of experience in this respect. However, one of the main questions here is whether Japan is ready for such a role.

When Japanese PM Fumio Kishida visited Ukraine earlier in March 2023, he became the first Japanese post-war leader to visit a warzone. Interestingly, this visit came at almost the same time as the visit by the

Chinese President, Xi Jinping, to Moscow, clearly outlining the priorities of the two nations. While Kishida was the last G7 leader to visit Ukraine, the fact that he skirted domestic political requirements (which require that plans for international travel be made public) clearly reflects the extent to which he was determined to make it to Ukraine.

Prime Minister Kishida is no stranger to high office. He holds the record for being Japan's longest-serving postwar foreign minister between 2012 and 2017. He also has extensive experience of working under Japan's former and longest-serving PM, Shinzo Abe, who was the brain-child behind the concept of the Free and Open Indo-Pacific (also known as the FOIP).

Kishida has continued with the FOIP and in a major policy speech during his visit to India, earlier in March last year, he outlined the "new four pillars" of cooperation for FOIP: principles for peace and rules for prosperity, addressing challenges in an Indo-Pacific way, multi-layered connectivity, and extending efforts for security and safe use of the "sea" to the "air". The Indo-Pacific region is critical for Japan as its economic prosperity and security depend on free trade in the region.[1]

To be fair to him, PM Kishida had the difficult job of filling in the shoes of his predecessor Yoshihide Suga, who was preceded by former PM Shinzo Abe (who was assassinated in July last year), but he seems to have eased into the role. Ever since he took over in October 2021, Kishida has been playing a proactive role in international affairs. He has pushed Japan's case in different parts of the globe. In late April to early May 2023, PM Kishida embarked on a four-country trip to Africa and during this trip, Japan pledged $500 million in assistance to Africa over the next three years. Of late, China has secured a major foothold in Africa and Tokyo under PM Kishida understands Africa's importance for Japan. Besides, under him, Tokyo envisages to be an intermediary between the G7 nations and the developing countries and has indicated that he "hoped to offer tangible forms of cooperation from the G7 to the developing countries in areas including energy and food security." In keeping with his promise, he invited the leaders of eight countries — Australia, Brazil, Comoros (African Union Chair), Cook Island (Pacific Islands Forum (PIF) Chair), India (G20 Presidency), Indonesia (ASEAN Chair),

---

[1] *MoFA* (Ministry of Foreign Affairs), Government of Japan, Policy Speech by Prime Minister KISHIDA Fumio, available at https://www.mofa.go.jp/fp/pc/page1e_000586. html accessed on 27th May 2023.

Republic of Korea and Vietnam — to the G7 Summit held in his hometown of Hiroshima in May 2023.

On the economic front, PM Kishida has been able to steer the Japanese economy to recovery after the hit it suffered in light of the outbreak of the coronavirus pandemic. In what is welcome news, Japan's GDP expanded at an annualised pace of 1.6% in the first three months of 2023, which was far above market expectations. It is worth noting here that Japan went through a technical recession at the end of last year.

PM Kishida had also set his eyes on improving Japan's ties with neighbours like South Korea. He had visited South Korea earlier in May 2023 (during the first visit to Seoul by a Japanese leader in 12 years) while the South Korean President had visited Japan earlier in March last year. The South Korean President was also invited to the G7 Summit in Hiroshima (which he attended) and this points to a new era in the relationship, which had deteriorated quite rapidly during the preceding times.

Foreign Policy Challenges for Japan

However, there are still a lot of challenges for Japan.

Japan had requested and received a waiver to purchase Russian oil above the $US 60 cap on purchases of Russian oil which had been agreed to by the G7 countries, Australia and the EU. Some Japanese companies are still doing business with Russia, in spite of its invasion of Ukraine. One such case is that of a consortium of Japanese companies which hold a 30% stake in the Sakhalin Oil and Gas Development Company, or SODECO, in the northeastern part of Russia. Russian President Vladimir Putin unilaterally announced a plan to establish a new operator for Russia's Sakhalin 1 project (earlier operated by Exxon Mobil). In spite of the Sakhalin project passing into the hands of the Russian government, Japan has decided to retain its stake.

Another challenge for Japan is that it is facing a critical situation when it comes to its energy security. This is because after the Fukushima nuclear disaster (in the wake of the March 11, 2011, earthquake), Japan has cut down on nuclear energy. At the same time, Japan is a net energy importer, importing close to 96% of its current energy consumption needs.

Then there is the China dilemma. While Japan faces a major challenge from China on the security front, it still has close economic ties with it. In addition, the Taiwan issue is like a ticking time bomb for Japan as Beijing has adopted a very belligerent posture after the visit by the then US House Speaker Nancy Pelosi to Taiwan in August 2022. China fired several missiles in its immediate aftermath and some of these landed in Japan's territorial waters and this represents a new worry for Japan. At the same time, PM Kishida has warned that "Ukraine may be the East Asia of tomorrow",[2] and this may well be true in case hostilities break out over Taiwan.

China has also been claiming the Japanese-controlled Senkaku islands (known as Diaoyu in China). Japan has also been trying to increase its options when it comes to its business interests in Southeast Asia. It has been trying to move away its lines of production from China to Southeast Asia.

North Korea presents another major challenge for Japan. Pyongyang in recent years and months has sent missiles flying over Japan and since the end of the term of the Trump Administration in the US, there has been no further talks between the US and North Korea. There has also been no progress on the issue of Japanese citizens abducted by North Korea. What further complicates the matter for Japan is that all these nations — North Korea, China and Russia — are nuclear-armed.

In addition, there is the issue of Japan's past. Will Japan's past catch up with its present-day forays? Japan's relations with its neighbours like China, South Korea and Taiwan have been strained on account of its past, and this is likely to play up during the upcoming years too. In the past, when former PM Shinzo Abe had visited the controversial Yasukuni Shrine in Tokyo, this has led to protests in its neighbouring countries as the Yasukuni Shrine is believed to house the spirits of Japan's war dead. Hence, PM Kishida will have to work extra hard to shed this historical baggage.

PM Kishida faces quite a few challenges on the domestic front as well.

A big challenge for Japan is on the demographic front. Japan has been grappling with a falling birth rate which will have severe repercussions on all fronts, especially on the economic and the security fronts.

In addition, there are various factions within the ruling LDP (Liberal Democratic Party) and these are all likely to put pressure on PM Kishida when it comes to policymaking, on both the domestic and international fronts.

---

[2] *VoA*, Japan PM: East Asia Could Be Next Ukraine, available at https://www.voanews.com/a/kishida-says-g7-should-show-strong-will-on-russia-s-ukraine-invasion/6918474.html accessed on 27th May 2023.

How is Japan Responding to These Challenges?

Under Prime Minister Kishida, Japan has announced a big increase in its defence budget. Spending on defence is projected to increase to 2% of its GDP in the next five years and this represents a big leap forward for Japan, especially since there is a strong resistance to militarism within the country. Japan's Defence Budget is expected to grow to 8.9 trillion yen by 2027.[3] Meanwhile, in response to the threats from China, the Japanese helicopter carriers *JS Izumo* and *JS Kaga* are being retrofitted to allow them to be able to launch the F-35B, the US Marine Corps variant of F-35 Joint Strike Fighter. This in itself is a major step forward for Japan.

These Japanese warships have also gone on advanced deployment in various parts of the Indo-Pacific. Japan will also be buying 400 Tomahawk missiles from the US to tackle emerging threats in its neighbourhood. It is also an influential member of the QUAD (Quadrilateral Security Dialogue) and a part of the Malabar naval exercises along with India, the US and Australia.

Meanwhile, in the draft edition of its defence white paper in 2023, Tokyo has expressed fears regarding increasing Russian and Chinese military activities in waters around the country, saying they seem "to clearly intend a show of force to our country." It also points out that China and Russia have conducted a total of five joint bomber flights near Japan since July 2019.[4]

Then, there is the threat from Russia. The two countries, Japan and Russia, have never signed a peace treaty after the Second World War and tensions between the two countries are likely to continue in the near future. PM Kishida has taken a stronger stand against Russia as opposed to former Japanese PM Shinzo Abe who tried to forge close ties with President Putin. In the past, Abe had also attended the opening ceremony of the Sochi Winter Olympics back in 2014. The two countries have a territorial dispute over what is known as the Northern Territories in Japan and the Southern Kurils in Russia.

---

[3] *Nikkei Asia*, Japan's G-7 test: Kishida pushes active foreign policy onto global stage, available at https://asia.nikkei.com/Spotlight/The-Big-Story/Japan-s-G-7-test-Kishida-pushes-active-foreign-policy-onto-global-stage accessed on 23rd May 2023.

[4] *Japan Times*, China may move up plan for 'world-class military,' Japan says in draft report, available at https://www.japantimes.co.jp/news/2023/05/24/national/defense-paper-draft-china-military/ accessed on 28th May 2023.

Can Japan Take the Lead Again?

Japan's successful hosting of the G7 Summit earlier in May last year shows that PM Kishida has come of age when it comes to the global stage. One of the highlights of this year's G7 Summit was the physical presence of Ukrainian President Zelensky. Japan has also been taking a more pro-active role when it comes to the situation in Ukraine. Earlier in February this year, Japan announced roughly US$5.5 billion of financial support to Ukraine. Tokyo's Ukraine-related assistance totalled US$7.1 billion dollars, and during his visit to the country earlier in March 2023, PM Kishida announced an additional 470 million dollars in bilateral grant aid.[5] Japan's role will also be important during the reconstruction phase of Ukraine as it has extensive experience in reconstruction activities, especially in the aftermath of natural disasters/conflict situations.

The G7 under Japan has also taken a strong stand when it comes to the human rights situation inside China. The G7 leaders' communique in May 2023 noted that "we will keep voicing our concerns about the human rights situation in China, including in Tibet and Xinjiang where forced labor is of major concern to us. We call on China to honour its commitments under the Sino-British Joint Declaration and the Basic Law, which enshrine rights, freedoms and a high degree of autonomy for Hong Kong."[6]

However, this led to a backlash from China and the Japanese Ambassador in China was summoned. This does not bode too well for Japan as in the past Tokyo has avoided going the whole hog against Beijing. This also underlines the dangers for Japan as it takes a more pro-active step in global affairs.

Though PM Kishida's home constituency is Hiroshima, he understands very well that Japan will need to shoulder the burden of its own security. The US under the Biden Administration has refused to get entangled in

---

[5]Government of Japan, Japan Continues to Stand with Ukraine, available at https://www.japan.go.jp/kizuna/2023/04/japan_continues_to_stand_with_ukraine.html#:~:text=In%20February%2C%20Japan%20announced%20roughly,assistance%20totaled%207.1%20billion%20dollars accessed on 27th May 2023.

[6]The White House, G7 Hiroshima Leaders' Communiqué, available at https://www.whitehouse.gov/briefing-room/statements-releases/2023/05/20/g7-hiroshima-leaders-communique/ accessed on 24th May 2023.

disputes where its own national security interests are not directly at stake, as seen in the case of Ukraine.

As opposed to China, Japan under PM Kishida has positioned itself as a stable democracy and a resilient economy on which Western countries can rely upon. As the G7 countries now want to de-risk from China, Japan's role will be crucial. Under PM Kishida, Japan has been playing a role commensurate with its clout as the world's third biggest economy.

What is Bringing Countries Like India, Japan and the US Closer?

Many years ago, former Japanese Prime Minister, Shinzo Abe, had noted in a landmark speech before the Indian Parliament (in August 2007) titled "Confluence of the Two Seas" that "the Pacific and the Indian Oceans are now bringing about a dynamic coupling as seas of freedom and of prosperity."

A series of factors are bringing these countries closer.

First, common interests in the Indo-Pacific region. This includes factors like freedom of navigation in this region, which is a major global economic artery. It has been estimated that nearly 36 million barrels of oil — which is close to about 40% of the world's oil supply and 64% of oil trade — pass through the Indian Ocean every single day.

Second, the fear that the US may not be able to provide the kind of security guarantees in the future as it had done in the past is also bringing these countries closer. While this is certainly not true, the US remains a deeply divided nation as seen in the last Presidential elections.

Third, each one of them has had run-ins with China in the recent past. While in the case of Japan, it has been China's aggressive actions in the Senkakus (which are claimed as Diaoyu by China), and in the case of India, it has been the Chinese incursions in its border region. For Australia, these exercises mark a leap of faith as it had close ties with China, especially in the economic domain, until the ties started unravelling earlier this year.

Fourth, India has set up a tri-services command in the strategically important Andaman and Nicobar islands, which are a choke point. Another factor that has played an important role in these developments is India's growing ties with the US. India has been buying a huge array of

US-made military hardware in recent times and US defence sales to India have skyrocketed to more than $20 billion now. The US also cannot ignore the fact that India is the world's biggest arms importer.

Challenges for the US

However, there are quite a few challenges as well and it is not going to be an easy path going ahead.

First, with the upcoming elections, it remains to be seen what kind of an approach the US takes towards China. While the Biden Administration had taken a very hardline approach towards Beijing, it remains to be seen if the new US administration will walk down the same path.

Second, since China is a member of the P5, the US requires China's cooperation in a wide variety of areas especially when it comes to Russia. In addition, with tensions flaring in the Middle East between the Israelis and the Palestinians and again the attacks by the Houthis, China's cooperation is important for the US.

Importance of Cooperation in the Maritime Arena

Joint Exercises between India, the US and Japan like the Malabar are very important, to tackle not only traditional security challenges but also non-traditional security challenges, in the Indo-Pacific. In the past, issues like piracy, civil war and others have posed new challenges for policymakers in the region.

As maritime democracies, it will be critical for these countries to walk the talk when it comes to the Malabar. In case any of these countries chicken out now, it may be difficult to resuscitate the Malabar in its present form. It is very clear that the maritime realm will see increased cooperation between the Malabar member countries as options on land are limited.

The maritime realm will be key as these countries seek to counter China's growing aggressiveness in the region. Beijing's coercive actions have been at full display when it comes to countries like the Philippines and also in some cases Vietnam and calls for a concerted strategy. Meanwhile, as part of its so-called "String of Pearls" strategy, Beijing has been developing or has helped develop a series of ports in countries like Sri Lanka (Hambantota), Pakistan (Gwadar), Bangladesh (Chittagong) and Myanmar (Kyaukpyu).

What are the Alternatives to the BRI?

What is needed are sustainable solutions which can take into account the environmental needs of the participating countries. The present model of infrastructure development is not sustainable. We have seen that rapid infrastructure development in many parts of the developing world is taking a toll on the ecological condition of these countries.

Japan already has a lot of experience in this respect as it has faced a big challenge after the Second World War. It was then that it employed innovative solutions to tackle the challenges. In addition, infrastructure development should not only be about roads, it should also be about railways. It is important for India's infrastructure development that the railways are also developed, especially as India is a country which has the highest number of people in the world.

For India, the main challenge is to uplift its own citizens. The government is undertaking huge economic reforms and it has been successful as well. However, if the government spends money on infrastructure outside India, it could be difficult for the government to recover its investments.

The best plan would therefore be for India, Japan and the US to work on their strengths and this need not be only about physical infrastructure, this could well extend to the digital sphere as well. However, the proof of the pudding will be in the eating as they say. This will take a concerted effort for India, Japan and the US to pull it off. However, the risks of not doing it are too great to bear

Another challenge for India is employment generation and hence investing in infrastructure outside India may not be immediately helpful for the government. As the US heads into an election year, it will be difficult for the US as well.

China's Economic Slowdown and its Possible Impact on the BRI

Reports are emerging from across the world which point out to the fact that China's economy now is at an inflection point. Growth rates have fallen (when compared to the last few years) and there is massive unemployment. At the same time, the real estate sector seems to be in a state of free fall and leading private sector firms like Evergrande and Country Garden are in the doldrums.

Barclays has already cut its forecast for China's 2023 gross domestic product (GDP) growth to 4.5% from 4.9%. At the same time, economic activity in China across sectors like retail sales, industrial output and investment failed to match expectations, thereby leading to concerns about a longer-lasting slowdown in growth.

So, What does This Mean for China's Neighbours?

It means that President Xi Jinping might show an increasing appetite for action on the external front since on the domestic front, he is clearly on a weak footing. Earlier in August 2023, China came out with a so-called "standard map" which includes parts of many countries and this has enraged these countries. In addition, this could mean that Japan and Taiwan could be on the crosshairs of China.

As already seen, in the aftermath of the release of treated radioactive water from the Fukushima nuclear plant by Japan into the Pacific Ocean in August last year, China created a ruckus. Among others, stones and eggs have been thrown at Japanese schools/establishments in China. This clearly proves that China will divert attention elsewhere when it comes to the economic front.

In addition, this would mean that Japan would need to boost its defences. Already the Kishida Administration has significantly increased the defence budget in light of threats from China, among others. The recent Cabinet reshuffle could also be a step in this direction as the foreign and defence ministers have been replaced.

With India too, China seems to be in no mood to relent. It is worth mentioning here that the two countries had fatal clashes in the summer of 2020, the first in almost 45 years. In addition, Xi Jinping cancelled his trip to the G20 Heads of State meeting in New Delhi in September last year and this clearly shows that it will ratchet up the pressure on other fronts.

With the ASEAN countries too, things seem to be no better. Beijing is involved in territorial disputes with many ASEAN countries. Already we see that there is a pushback when it comes to the various actors in Southeast Asia when it comes to China's infrastructure projects.

China's Advantages

However, on the other hand, China is investing in cutting-eage industries like semi-conductors and electric cars and these industries are likely to gain momentum in the times ahead.

Another important factor for China is that it does not have to go through an election cycle and therefore can take tough decisions. In addition, with its huge population, there is enough domestic demand when it comes to the economy. China is also a member of the RCEP and hence it will be difficult to completely cut off China from the global economy.

Challenges

However, China has its own set of challenges.

These include a falling and ageing population. Though Chinese authorities have done away with the one-child policy, there are few takers for a second child.

Chinese President Xi Jinping has already fired his Foreign Minister Qin Gang and two top leaders of its People's Liberation Army Rocket Force (PLARF), which handles the Chinese nuclear arsenal. This clearly shows that not all is well on the domestic front. In addition, the central government has called on the country's richest provinces — Guangdong, Jiangsu, Zhejiang, Shandong, Henan and Sichuan which account for roughly 40% of economic output — to help the other provinces.

Long-Term Impact

The long-term impact of this will be that most of the countries (except countries which are close allies of China like North Korea and Russia) will decouple from China and the Chinese economy. Earlier, India's leading trade partner was China but now it has been replaced by the US and this is certainly good news. Moreover, India, Japan, the US and Australia are a part of the QUAD and these countries are also witnessing a remarkable deal of cooperation on the economic front.

While the failure of the Chinese economy is certainly news for the global economy, this is certainly not bad news. It means that there will now be two global economic orders — one would be the Sino-centric economic world order and the other one would be the non-Sinocentric world.

In March 2023, Chinese President XI Jinping was elected for an unprecedented third term as the President of China. This means that he has subsumed all powers and has become the most powerful leader after Mao Zedong.

Will China Come Out of This Slump?

It is difficult to say now if China will come out of this slump. We will have to adopt a wait-and-watch approach. Meanwhile, there have also been rumours floating around with regard to the health of the Chinese President with some reports last year talking about him suffering from cerebral aneurysm.

China could very well be a victim of its own progress. Local governments are trying to spend heavily on infrastructure building but there seem to be no takers for these projects. In addition, people are also spending less because of the pandemic years and this has brought down demand. The zero-COVID policy followed by Beijing seems to have had disastrous lessons. Countries like India, Japan and others would do well to learn lessons from China's economic slowdown and take appropriate steps while there is time.

What China also needs to worry about is falling into what is known as the middle-income trap where it will grow old before it becomes rich. This, in itself, will be a big challenge.

Time To Take A Call

New Delhi launched its "Act-East Policy" in the early 1990s in the wake of the dissolution of the former Soviet Union — this policy aimed at re-establishing India's historical ties with the countries of Southeast Asia and East Asia. Another reason for the outlining of this policy was for the rapid development of India's Northeastern region, which has lagged behind other parts of the country in most development indicators.

Now, as the fighting increases in Myanmar, its "Act-East Policy" is under threat and hence it is time for New Delhi to take a call on where its priorities and interests lie in Myanmar. Sooner or later, the fighting will end in Myanmar and it will be in New Delhi's interests to have channels of communication open with all the warring parties.

Covid and Afterwards

Another factor which has to be noted is that for both the recipient countries and also for China, the scenario has changed completely after COVID. The supply lines in China were disrupted badly and there will be no going back to the pre-COVID levels, it seems. China's priorities also have changed.

All this has put paid on China's global ambitions at least for the time being. The G7 at its Hiroshima Summit also noted that "deliver our goal of mobilizing $600 billion in financing for quality infrastructure through the Partnership for Global Infrastructure Investment (PGII)".[7]

The same communiqué also noted that "coordinate our approach to economic resilience and economic security that is based on diversifying and deepening partnerships and de-risking, not de-coupling".[8]

Backlash Among Local Populace

Then there is the issue of backlash among the local populace when it comes to the BRI projects even though most of the governments have been very open towards tying up with the BRI.

The question is in many of these cases, the projects were initiated without taking the local sensibilities into question and hence the opposition.

What India, Japan and the US should also try is to provide sustainable alternatives in the field of connectivity and this is what will set them apart in the field of connectivity. Already, as we have seen, especially in the summer of 2024, temperatures have risen to unprecedented levels in Southeast Asia and South Asia.

Hence, the solutions also need to be innovative before the results become even more disastrous.

In addition, apart from Japan, India and the US, European countries could also pitch in when it comes to the Indo-Pacific since they also have a common interest in ensuring a FOIP.

Developments in Myanmar and Impact on India and Japan

The civil war in Myanmar seems to be spreading and some of it is spilling over into the Northeastern part of India, especially into the states of Manipur and Mizoram. At the same time, Japan had been putting in huge

---

[7]The White House, G7 Hiroshima Summit Joint Statement, https://www.whitehouse.gov/briefing-room/statements-releases/2023/05/20/g7-hiroshima-leaders-communique/.

[8]*Ibid.*

investments into Myanmar in the wake of the opening up of the country but that has taken a turn for the worse now with the current developments.

Japanese companies have had big investments in Myanmar, which have had to be put on the backburner now. Tokyo had an early foothold in the ASEAN region which started with the "Fukuda Doctrine" of 1977 outlining the nature of Japan's cooperation with the ASEAN nations, but it seems China has now got a bigger hold in the region. Indonesia has started the high-speed railway between Bandung and Jakarta, with assistance from China.

A high-profile Japanese company which left Myanmar after the coup was the Japanese beverage giant Kirin, which sold its 51% stake in a joint venture, Myanmar Brewery. On the other hand, some Japanese businesses have chosen to stay put and are waiting for the crisis to blow over, but it is easier said than done. Japan had invested heavily in the Thilawa Special Economic Zone outside Yangon.

India has been successful in building ties with the government in Myanmar, but now things have changed after the takeover of power by the junta leader Min Aung Hlaing, who ousted the elected government in a coup in February 2021. For some Japanese companies, Myanmar seemed as the "last frontier" of Asia. That certainly seems to be changing now as the civil war intensifies.

What is in It for India?

For India, there is a lot at stake.

First, Myanmar is India's gateway to Southeast Asia and to the ASEAN region as a whole and it has a land border with that country. New Delhi has indicated that it would seal that border, but it is not an easy task given the terrain of the region, which is mountainous and gets a lot of rainfall. India has already scrapped the FMR (Free Movement Regime), which allowed any member of a hill tribe and a citizen of either India or Myanmar, and residing "within 16 km of the border on either side, to cross on the production of a border pass, usually valid for a year, and stay up to two weeks per visit."

Second, India had a lot of investments in Myanmar, especially in the field of infrastructure with projects like the Kaladan Multi Modal Transport Corridor Project and the India–Myanmar–Thailand trilateral highway. These are surely going to run into difficult ground in the times ahead as there seems to be no immediate end to the ongoing civil strife in the country.

Third, India had invested heavily in projects like the Sittwe River Port in Myanmar and all these projects will now be hanging fire now, in light of the current situation.

What Can India and Japan do?

Here, India and Japan need to form a common approach when dealing with Myanmar. This year is going to be very difficult when it comes to the situation in Myanmar. The silver lining seems to be the fact that the recent elections in Bangladesh have brought back the Awami League to power and hence this is one country where India and Japan can pool their efforts and resources, till the time the situation cools down in Myanmar.

The China Factor

India and Japan also need to worry about the China factor in the relationship. The Chinese have long helped the insurgent groups in Myanmar as a means of gaining leverage in the country. This is something India and Japan have not done in the past and cannot do in the future too, but China would surely try to jettison any plans by India and Japan to make their position stronger in Myanmar.

Already it seems that the anti-government ultras have wrested control of some parts of the country, which, however, is in no mood to give up control of the country. They have some big and powerful friends in the form of China and Russia, which are keen on maintaining their influence in the country.

Since the military coup, Japan has stopped giving new aid to Myanmar and has called on the coup leaders to stop the violence. However, its stand has been much weaker than that of the US European Union and others. However, totally cutting off contact with the government in Myanmar could also be risky as this could allow China to gain leverage in the country to the detriment of India and Japan.

It was in 2013 that former Japanese Prime Minister Shinzo Abe visited Myanmar, and he brought executives from about 40 companies and organisations with him. For Japan, Myanmar is important for what is known in Japan as the "Thailand plus one" — a strategy to extend supply chains developed in Thailand and seek new low-cost production sites in other ASEAN nations. This strategy has come into increasing focus in the wake of the disruption in the Japanese supply lines in the wake of the outbreak of the coronavirus pandemic.

That strategy certainly seems to be under threat now, given the present happenings in Myanmar. Hence, it would be useful for India and Japan to draw up a combined strategy to tackle the unforeseen situation in Myanmar and wait for the situation to blow over.

The Attacks on International Shipping by the Houthis: How will It Impact India and Japan

The recent attacks on commercial shipping in the Red Sea by Houthi rebels from Yemen promise to turn into a big danger for both the Indian and Japanese economies, especially as both of them are energy-deficient countries. Japan and India have been collaborating for a long time, in the field of maritime security. It was in September 1999, that a Japanese-owned, Panama-registered ship, the MV Alondra Rainbow, was hijacked by pirates, who were later apprehended by the Indian Coast Guard.

This will be a litmus test for both India and Japan as well as other countries as attacks of such a scale and nature have not happened earlier. The Indian Navy's MARCOS naval commandos helped rescue a cargo ship "MV Lila Norfolk" with all 21 crew members, including Indians, that was hijacked near the coast of Somalia.

While the Houthis insist that they are "targeting vessels which are Israeli-owned, flagged or operated, or are heading to Israeli ports", however, in many cases, vessels which have no connection with Israel have been attacked.

What is at Stake for India?

There are many things at stake for India here.

For one, India depends hugely on oil imports from the Gulf countries. Though the Houthi rebels are backed by Iran, New Delhi cannot blame Iran directly it has launched a series of infrastructure projects in Iran. Already India has stopped oil imports from Iran in light of Western-led sanctions on Iran. To counter China's China–Pakistan Economic Corridor (CPEC) in Pakistan and the BRI (as a whole), Iran remains an important country for India.

Second, India has not joined the international coalition against the Houthis, known as "Operation Prosperity Guardian." Besides, the US, it brings together, countries like the United Kingdom, Bahrain, Canada, France, Italy, Netherlands, Norway, Seychelles and Spain. In addition, its relations with the US seem to have hit a rough patch in recent times.

Third, India has stakes in the region as a huge number of expatriates live and work in the Middle East and make a big contribution to its economy via remittances. Any increase in oil prices will have an impact on the domestic situation.

Fourth, it will be a test case for the Indian Navy. Earlier it had successfully rescued its own citizens along with other countries from war-torn Yemen in 2015. The Indian Ministry of External Affairs noted that "we attach very high importance to freedom of navigation, and free movement of commercial shipping. It is an evolving situation and we are looking at all aspects of it".

Indian External Affairs Minister Dr S Jaishankar visited Iran in January 2024 and conveyed New Delhi's genuine concerns to Iran. Terming the attacks on ships in the vicinity of India as a matter of "grave concern" to the international community, Dr Jaishankar underlined that "this is a matter of great concern to the international community. Obviously, it also has a direct bearing on India's energy and economic interests. This fraught situation is not to the benefit of any party and this must be clearly recognised."[9]

What is at Stake for Japan

Many Japanese shipping firms like Nippon Yusen, a Japanese firm also known as NYK Line, and Mitsui O.S.K. Lines have decided to temporarily alter the course of their vessels to and from Europe to avoid the Red Sea and so has Kawasaki Kisen Kaisha, or K Line. In addition, Ocean Network Express has switched to the one around the Cape of Good Hope.

At the same time, the Japanese MoFA in a statement noted that "Japan condemns the continued interference by the Houthis with the rights and freedoms of navigation in the waters around the Arabian Peninsula, particularly in the Red Sea. Furthermore, Japan supports the determination of

---

[9]Ministry of External Affairs, Government of India, Joint Press Statement by EAM, Dr. S. Jaishankar with Minister of Foreign Affairs of Iran, https://www.mea.gov.in/outoging-visit-detail.htm?37513/Joint+Press+Statement+by+EAM+Dr+S+Jaishankar+with+Minister+of+Foreign+Affairs+of+Iran.

the US and relevant countries to fulfill its responsibility in ensuring the free and safe navigation of vessels. To this end, we understand that this action was a measure aimed at preventing the further deterioration of the situation."[10]

The Road Ahead

Now, things have changed with the start of military operations against the Houthis by the US/UK recently. However, this is not likely to dramatically alter things on ground as the Houthis have been able to withstand similar attacks in the past. However, this is surely going to drive up the price of oil. A joint statement in the aftermath of the airstrikes notes that "In response to continued illegal, dangerous, and destabilizing Houthi attacks against vessels, including commercial shipping, transiting the Red Sea, the armed forces of the US and United Kingdom, with support from the Netherlands, Canada, Bahrain, and Australia, conducted joint strikes in accordance with the inherent right of individual and collective self-defense".

New Delhi and Tokyo along with countries like the US will have to ensure that things do not go out of hand as they have immense stakes in the region. The Indian Navy has a big presence in the region while the JMSDF base in Djibouti. Both the countries, just like other countries, have seen their economies rebound after the hit in the wake of coronavirus and hence cannot afford yet another crisis.

India's Relations with Countries in China's Neighbourhood

New Delhi would also do well to improve its relations with countries in China's neighbourhood, especially countries like Mongolia and the Central Asian Republics. In addition, through the "Vaccine *Maitri* (Friendship)" program, India had already been reaching out to a host of countries in the neighbourhood by supplying Indian-made coronavirus vaccines at the peak of the pandemic.

---

[10]Ministry of Foreign Affairs of Japan, Joint Strikes against the Houthis by the United States and the United Kingdom available at https://www.mofa.go.jp/press/release/pressite_000001_00110.html.

What is certain is that New Delhi will now have to find out what China meant to achieve through this intrusion, in order to prevent the next intrusion. It will also be worthwhile to analyse what lies ahead for the wider spectrum of Sino-Indian ties in light of this aggression from China.

The best thing for New Delhi to do is to prepare plans to advance. It may also be better to spring a surprise or two on China. This will, however, depend on a host of factors including political resolve in India. Till that time, as they say, "eternal vigilance is the price of peace".

The Future of the BRI

The future of the BRI will depend on a host of factors. This includes the domestic conditions prevalent in China since this will be the main issue behind the funding process.

China may also try to take a relook at the same of the projects. However, the countries involved in BRI are also wary of the increasing burden when it comes to the economic front vis-a-vis China. Some of them, like Sri Lanka, were barely able to avoid getting entangled in a never-ending cycle of loans.

It will also depend on other factors like how long President Xi Jinping stays in power in China. There seems to be a power struggle among various groups within the Communist Party in China and that does not bode well for the country as a whole.

What Happens If India, Japan and the US do not Provide an Alternative?

In that case, countries across the world, especially those in the Global South, which are lagging behind in infrastructure may come under the trap of China and the Chinese BRI. In terms of infrastructure development, we have to see how the Chinese have built up infrastructure in parts of the country like Tibet, which shares borders with India. In addition, they have built up border villages in the remote Himalayan border areas, something which may have dual use in times of conflict and this is something that India needs to be careful about.

In addition, one of the main reasons for the BRI is to send the finished goods from China to other parts of the world, including Central Asia. This means that China is actually dumping its finished goods on different world markets and this is something that countries across the world need to understand. Most countries across the world are selling raw materials to China and buying finished goods from China and this is a very dangerous proposition, in economic terms.

Demographic Crisis in China

One of the serious issues is the demographic crisis in China which means that in the short and long terms, it will be impossible for China to sustain the current levels of growth with this kind of population implosion and this is one of the key reasons China has been looking at the world beyond its shores to drive demand.

However, how these countries respond to the BRI will also depend on how the domestic situation develops in these countries. The decision of the current Japanese Prime Minister Fumio Kishida to step down has brought a whole lot of issues into focus. One of them is the infighting within the LDP over the series of scandals that have dogged the party for some time now. The party and the Prime Minister seem to have been unable to get rid of the same.

What does It Mean for Japan as a Whole?

This means that Japan could be pushed into the same cycle of revolving door Prime Ministers as had happened in the past before the time of former Japanese Prime Minister Shinzo Abe.

While Shinzo Abe had been at the helm for 8 years after he stepped down, Yoshihide Suga had taken over as the Prime Minister, but he could stay only for a year in office. After Yoshihide Suga stepped down, PM Kishida had taken over, but with the stepping back of PM Kishida, things seem to be back to square one for Japan.

Highlights of the Kishida Era

During the term of PM Kishida, he worked hard to strengthen ties with the US. Also, the most important factor for the Kishida-led Japan was his increasing focus on strengthening the defence of Japan. Under Kishida's watch, Japan has decided to increase its defence budget to 2% of its GDP by 2027.

This is a big leap forward for Japan as in the past the Japanese constitution expressly prohibits it from spending a huge amount on its defence. In addition, the Japanese Parliament has also passed laws which will allow the export of the fighters jointly produced by Japan with Italy and Britain, to third countries and this in itself is a big development.

The recent decision of the Japanese government to give cabinet approval to the export of a next-generation fighter jet (being jointly developed with Italy and Britain) points to a new era in Japan's security outlook. This marks a significant development, especially in the wake of the state visit of the Japanese PM to the US earlier in April this year, which was the first visit by a Japanese PM to the US in 9 years. Washington has been preoccupied in other parts of the world and would like to see Japan take a more prominent role with respect to its security and Tokyo has already expressed its wish to be a "global partner" of the US.

The Global Combat Air Program, or GCAP, is a joint effort between Japan, the United Kingdom, and Italy which aims at developing an advanced fighter jet to replace ageing fleets. Initially, Japan was working on a domestic design known as the F-X, which was later merged with the British–Italian Tempest program in December 2022.

Technically, Japan can sell these latest generation fighter jets to countries like India, since it has signed defence deals with India. However, the devil will lie in the details as in the past the deal for the sale of ShinMaywa US2 amphibious aircraft from Japan to India never went through for a host of reasons.

However, this could also pave the way for future collaboration between India and Japan in the not-too-distant future as New Delhi is looking at a rapid indigenisation of its defence weaponry.

So, What does It Mean for Japan?

It means that Japan is slowly heading to a forward-looking defence posture which would have been unimaginable in the not-too-distant past. Japan will soon become the third biggest military spender in the world after the US and China with the increase of its military spending to 2% of its GDP.

Meanwhile, China's growing military prowess has Tokyo worried, especially as Beijing claims the Japanese-held Senkaku islands. China now has the biggest navy in terms of numbers and this is a big challenge for Japan. In addition, Japan also faces a threat on the northern front from

Russia and also from North Korea. Many a time in the past, North Korea has sent missiles flying over Japan. Hence, Japan's security scenario is really precarious as it faces dangers from three nuclear-armed antagonistic neighbours and Tokyo therefore needs to lay stress on its own defences.

Challenges

However, on the flip side, this could lead to an outcry from its neighbours and this could once again reignite old tensions in the region. Japan has indicated that it will export the aircraft only to countries with which it has already signed defence agreements and which are not engaged in conflicts.

However, this could be problematic since countries could enter a war after buying the fighter planes. In addition, this could lead to tensions between the LDP and its coalition partner, the Komeito, though as of now the two parties have already come to a conclusion.

In addition, we will have to wait and watch which way the US elections proceed. In case Donald Trump were to come back to power in the US, he could make new demands from Japan and the question remains how far would Japan be willing to go to please a Trump Administration, in case it were to come back to power.

However, only the export of fighter jets may not be enough as Japan is prevented by law from participating in offensive military operations. In addition, this may put more pressure on Japan in the future to participate in military operations across the world. What in case hostilities break out over Taiwan? Would Japan be willing to participate in the same?

Tough Questions for Japan

On the other hand, since this aircraft is being developed by Italy, Britain and Japan together, Tokyo could be considered as an unreliable partner in case it were to jettison plans to export the fighter.

However, what this means is that it is certainly the dawn of a new era for Japan, an era which started during the time of former Japanese Prime Minister Shinzo Abe under whom the Japanese Parliament passed laws that now allow the SDF (Self Defense Force) to come to the aid of its allies like the US even when Japan is not directly under attack.

However, on the positive side, it will give a fillip to Japan's domestic defence industry which has now been relegated to the sidelines. The global arms market is huge by any standards.

This may also open the doors for more defence exports from Japan to other countries. There are many nations, especially in Southeast Asia, which have borne the brunt of aggression from China, especially countries like the Philippines. Japan has already been giving military equipment to countries like the Philippines.

However, there is still time since these jets are not expected to come into service by 2035. What is certain, though, is that there will be no going back for Japan now that it has agreed to turn a corner. Decisions in Japan take time, but this one marks a major step forward for Japan.

Other Changes in India and the US

Meanwhile, Prime Minister Modi has taken charge in India after the results of the General Elections held earlier in May/June this year. However, what may preoccupy him is the fact that though he has come to power (for the third time) the ruling Bharatiya Janata Party did not get a majority on its own and now needs to depend on coalition partners for support. This will stymie his efforts to take big-time decisions.

In addition, with the elections coming in the US, many things will depend on the results of the same. In case former President Donald Trump were to come back to power, things will look different from what might happen if Kamala Harris were to become President.

How Will the Russia–Ukraine War Impact China's BRI?

In the case of the Russia–Ukraine war, China has undoubtedly taken the side of Russia by supplying weapons and armaments to a beleaguered Russia as it seeks to hold on to the territory it had seized earlier. Meanwhile, Russia is also battling a Ukrainian advance on its Kursk region and this is a major step by Ukraine which will help it turn the tide of the battle when it comes to the war.

However, this will also impact the Chinese push, especially when it comes to the BRI. This is because the attention of the world has moved away from the infrastructure front. Many countries in the Global South are suffering from food crisis as a result of this war (as Ukraine is one of the leading global producers of wheat). Prices of wheat-based products have increased in the wake of fighting between Ukraine and Russia.

The fight between Ukraine and Russia has also impacted the security situation in Eastern Europe and beyond. Thousands of people studying/working in Ukraine have been forced to go back to their own countries, putting a strain on the economies of these countries. In addition, due to the conflict in the Middle East, oil prices have risen, thereby putting a strain on the economies of many countries. India has been lucky in a way, as it has been able to import cheap Russian oil owing to its good relations with Russia, but not all countries have been that lucky as Western nations have put an embargo on the import of Russian energy. This will also forever change the energy basket of some countries like Germany, which had till now been relying on cheap Russian energy imports.

Economic Developments

It seems that the economy of countries across the world has been beset by a whole range of tensions and pulls and pressures and this is likely to have an impact on the infrastructure-building process in these countries. One of the biggest challenges is the outbreak of the coronavirus pandemic and in the aftermath of the same, countries across the world have suffered a severe economic hit.

While the economies of some of the countries have bounced back (after the outbreak of COVID), there are still issues with many countries and this is why infrastructure development may not be the top priority for many of the countries involved.

Will China Continue to Pour Money into the BRI?

Will China continue to pour money into the BRI? May not be on such a big scale as has happened before the outbreak of coronavirus and therein lies the challenge. In some countries, there are security concerns as well as in Pakistan where the inauguration of the Gwadar airport has been delayed due to security concerns.

Then there are issues like the US elections — It is quite possible that China will wait to see which way the wind is blowing before taking a call on the infrastructure front.

The Way Forward for India, Japan and the US On the Infrastructure Front

The idea is for India, Japan and the US to do things differently and therein lies the catch. The challenge for these three countries is that they have not worked together in the field of infrastructure development, though have worked together in other fields like disaster relief and also in the field of defence. This will entail collaboration between these three countries in a manner that has not happened earlier.

Second, another big challenge is how to provide funding for such massive infrastructure projects. Here, something similar to the AIIB (The Asian Infrastructure Investment Bank) may have to be developed. While we have the IMF (International Monetary Front) and the World Bank, they do not exclusively deal with the area of infrastructure.

Third, while Japan has the expertise since it has been building infrastructure in many parts of the world, especially in Southeast Asia, the US and India do not have this kind of experience.

So, it is very clear that while India, Japan and the US have no past experience or history of collaborating in the field of infrastructure, this is the right time for them to begin doing the same. If the countries, especially from the Global South are left at the mercy of the China-led BRI, the results could be disastrous not only for these countries but also for other countries in their neighbourhood and also for India, Japan and the US. What is most important to note here is that India, Japan and the US are democratic countries and the democratic world should provide an alternative to the China-led BRI when it comes to the infrastructure front. As they say, "a stitch in time saves nine".

Index